KOREA

IN

WORLD

HISTORY

FRONT COVER: Kwanghwamun Plaza in downtown Seoul, the approach to the Kyŏngbok Palace, with statues of Admiral Yi Sunsin, Korea's greatest war hero (foreground) and King Sejong the Great, who presented his people with their Han'gŭl alphabet in 1446 (nearer the palace gate). The palace faces south, protected by the Pukhan Mountain Range to the north.

BACK COVER: Downtown Seoul looking southward over districts that once comprised the heart of the walled royal capital.

Key Issues in Asian Studies, No. 10

AAS Resources for Teaching About Asia

KOREA

IN

WORLD

HISTORY

DONALD N. CLARK

Association for Asian Studies, Inc.
825 Victors Way, Suite 310
Ann Arbor, MI 48108 USA
www.asian-studies.org

KEY ISSUES IN ASIAN STUDIES
A series edited by Lucien Ellington, University of Tennessee at Chattanooga

"Key Issues" booklets complement the Association for Asian Studies' teaching journal, *Education About Asia*—a practical teaching resource for secondary school, college, and university instructors, as well as an invaluable source of information for students, scholars, libraries, and those who have an interest in Asia.

Formed in 1941, the Association for Asian Studies (AAS)—the largest society of its kind, with close to 8,000 members worldwide—is a scholarly, non-political, non-profit professional association open to all persons interested in Asia.

For further information, please visit www.asian-studies.org

Copyright © 2012 by the Association for Asian Studies, Inc.

Published by the Association for Asian Studies, Inc. All Rights Reserved. Written permission must be secured to use or reproduce any part of this book.

For orders or inquiries, please contact:
    Association for Asian Studies, Inc.
    825 Victors Way, Suite 310
    Ann Arbor, MI 48108 USA
    Tel: (734) 665-2490
    Fax: (734) 665-3801
    www.asian-studies.org

Library of Congress Cataloging-in-Publication Data

Clark, Donald N.

Korea in world history / Donald N. Clark.

    p. cm. — (Key issues in Asian studies ; no. 10)

Includes bibliographical references.

ISBN 978-0-924304-66-8 (pbk. : alk. paper) 1. Korea—History. I. Title.

DS916.C59 2012

951.9—dc23

2011042502

The Korea Foundation has provided financial assistance for the undertaking of this publication project.

*For Franke Johnson
and the teachers of the
National Consortium for
Teaching About Asia (NCTA)*

About "Key Issues in Asian Studies"

Key Issues in Asian Studies (KIAS) is a series of booklets engaging major cultural and historical themes in the Asian experience. *KIAS* booklets complement the Association for Asian Studies' teaching journal, *Education About Asia*, and serve as vital educational materials that are both accessible and affordable for classroom use.

"Key Issues" booklets tackle broad subjects or major events in an introductory but compelling style appropriate for survey courses. Although authors of the series have distinguished themselves as scholars as well as teachers, the prose style employed in *KIAS* booklets is accessible for broad audiences. This series is particularly intended for teachers and undergraduates at two- and four-year colleges as well as advanced high school students and secondary school teachers engaged in teaching Asian studies in a comparative framework and anyone with an interest in Asia.

For further information about *Key Issues in Asian Studies* booklets, *Education About Asia*, or the Association for Asian Studies, visit www.asian-studies.org.

Prospective authors interested in *Key Issues in Asian Studies* or *Education About Asia* are encouraged to contact:

> Lucien Ellington
> University of Tennessee at Chattanooga
> Tel: (423) 425-2118; Fax (423) 425-5441
> E-Mail: Lucien-Ellington@utc.edu

"Key Issues" booklets available from AAS:

> *Traditional China in Asian and World History* by Tansen Sen and Victor Mair
>
> *Zen Past and Present* by Eric Cunningham
>
> *Japan and Imperialism, 1853–1945* by James L. Huffman
>
> *Japanese Popular Culture and Globalization* by William M. Tsutsui
>
> *Global India circa 100 CE: South Asia in Early World History* by Richard H. Davis
>
> *Caste in India* by Diane Mines
>
> *Understanding East Asia's Economic "Miracles"* by Zhiqun Zhu
>
> *Political Rights in Post-Mao China* by Merle Goldman
>
> *Gender, Sexuality, and Body Politics in Modern Asia* by Michael Peletz

About the Author

DONALD CLARK is part of a three-generation Presbyterian missionary family whose members spent a combined total of 216 years in Korea between 1902 and 1973. His own childhood in Seoul planted interests that turned into a career in Korean Studies, starting with Peace Corps service in the 1960s. This was followed by graduate degrees at Harvard University in the 1970s and thirty-three years teaching about Asia in the liberal arts environment of Trinity University in San Antonio, Texas, where he is now Murchison Professor of History. At Trinity, Professor Clark also co-chairs the East Asian Studies at Trinity ("EAST") Program and anchors the university's participation in the National Consortium for Teaching about Asia (NCTA), funded by the Freeman Foundation.

Photograph of Donald Clark by Sophie Shrem.

Professor Clark's books include general histories as well as specialized works on the history of Seoul (one co-written with his father Allen Clark and another with James Grayson), the history of Christianity in Korea, and Korea's relations with the West, including *Missionary Photography in Korea: Encountering the West through Christianity* (Korea Society, 2009) and *Living Dangerously in Korea: The Western Experience, 1900–1950* (EastBridge, 2003). He is currently writing a book about American diplomats on the Front Lines of the Cold War in Korea during the 1950s and early sixties.

CONTENTS

Acknowledgments and Preface

Korea in World History is for general readers, including teachers and students who want to include the story of the Korean people in broader coverage of East Asia in the schools. The scope is ambitious for such a small booklet. Korea's story spans thousands of years, and much longer histories struggle to give the various dynasties and periods their due. Sometimes Korea gets overlooked because there is not enough time to "cover" it in depth. The *Key Issues in Asian Studies* series offers this volume as an answer to that problem—making it possible to include Korea where otherwise it might remain all-but-unknown.

For many years my home campus, Trinity University, has offered a series of seminars to teachers as part of the National Consortium for Teaching about Asia (NCTA), generously funded by the Freeman Foundation. As the coordinator of Trinity's NCTA seminars who is also a Korea specialist I have found that teachers in the program reflect a public curiosity about Korea and an eagerness to learn where it fits in East Asia and the world. This booklet is the product of that experience, covering the basic history with an emphasis on more recent times, adding discussions about colonialism, the cold war, and ongoing tensions with North Korea, or more properly the Democratic People's Republic of Korea (DPRK).

I am grateful to Lucien Ellington, founding editor of *Education About Asia*, for encouraging me to write this book as part of the *Key Issues in Asian Studies* series. Lucien is a tireless advocate for Asian studies in the schools and a shining example of the influence that an individual can have on an entire profession through vision and hard work. At the Association for Asian Studies, Jonathan Wilson has guided the book throughout the writing and production process, and I am grateful to him for his patience and professional skill. Thanks also to Janet Opdyke for her editing, to my Trinity faculty colleague Diane Smith for the maps, to Eunice Herrington of the Trinity History Department for editorial help, and to Franke Johnson for her leadership and counsel in organizing Trinity's NCTA seminars and to successive groups of NCTA teachers for their inspiration and enthusiastic responses to learning and teaching about Korea in the classroom.

Editor's Introduction

The Koreas are important to both the U.S. and the world, but never-the-less usually do not receive the attention they deserve in our schools and universities. Many educated Americans are aware that the U.S. participated in a war on the peninsula in the mid-20th century, that the Republic of Korea (South Korea) has one of the world's larger and more successful economies, and that the intentions and policies of the Democratic Peoples' Republic of Korea (North Korea) often constitute potential and actual threats to national, regional, and possibly, international security. Others have some knowledge of the Republic of Korea's "educational miracle" that rivals its economic success story, and of the ROK's evolution from authoritarian to democratic government.

What students in our educational institutions do not usually learn is a deeper context for the disparate understandings they have concerning Korea; knowledge rooted in the long history of the peninsula and the varied interactions of Koreans with the rest of the world and with each other. Despite having studied Japan for well over a decade, before first meeting Donald Clark in 1996 during an Asian Studies Development Program (ASDP) Korea institute and study tour, I lacked any broad understanding of Korea. Don, along with Edward Shultz, were my first Korea teachers and I am forever grateful for the opportunities they provided me through their creative work, to learn and think in systematic and reflective ways about Korean history, culture, and contemporary institutions.

Since we first met, Don—in his articles in *Education About Asia* and through his National Consortium for Teaching Asia (NCTA) institutes and telecast broadcasts—has assisted teachers and professors throughout the U.S. in learning about a culture that deserves study as a distinct culture and not just a place that is important because of other neighboring states or powers that have interests in the region. My appreciation of Don, as a scholar and a teacher, is echoed by numerous people who have worked with him throughout the years.

Don was the ideal teacher/scholar to write this *Key Issues* volume and two general characteristics of the work are exceptional. In a brief volume, Don manages to articulately make the case for the importance of Korea, provide an excellent overview of Korean history and culture and its world importance, and focus upon the post-war Koreas in such a way that students will better understand contemporary affairs. As important, given that *Key Issues in Asian Studies* is intended to be, first and foremost, a pedagogical tool, Don's clear prose is highly accessible for both high school and university survey students.

In addition to Don's hard work, this volume would not have been possible without the useful comments of Suzy Kim and Constance Vidor who served as manuscript reviewers. As always, I am also deeply grateful to the AAS Editorial Board and Editorial Board Chair, Martha Selby in particular, and to AAS Publications Manager, Jonathan Wilson, and AAS Publications Coordinator, Gudrun Patton, for their strong support of pedagogical scholarship projects such as *Key Issues in Asian Studies* and *Education About Asia*.

Lucien Ellington

Series Editor, Key Issues in Asian Studies

TIMELINE

668: Unification of most of Korea under the Silla kingdom based in Kyŏngju.

918: Founding of the Koryŏ kingdom under King Wang Gŏn, with his capital at Kaesŏng. Silla submits in 935.

958: Koryŏ adopts the Chinese civil service examination system, giving rise to a new emphasis on classical Confucian ethics and government.

993–1018: After two invasions by the Khitans in the Liao region, Koryŏ reasserts control north to the Yalu River.

1196: Military officers seize political control in the Koryŏ kingdom and rule until 1258.

1231–59: In several incursions, the Mongol empire forces Korea to accept its overlordship.

1392: General Yi Sŏnggye overthrows the Koryŏ regime and founds the Chosŏn dynasty.

1396: Seoul is founded as the dynastic capital.

1446: King Sejong grants his people the simple alphabet known as *han'gŭl*.

1592–98: The Japanese invasion of Korea, or the Imjin War, as it is known in Korea.

1627: Manchu invasion of Korea.

1636: After a second Manchu invasion, Korea submits to the rising Qing dynasty in China.

1866: Last great persecution of Catholic Christians in Korea.

1876: Japan sends gunboats to Kanghwa Island on Korea's west coast. Koreans agree to their first modern diplomatic treaty. Other treaties follow with the United States (1882) and other world powers.

1895: Japan wins the Sino-Japanese War. China is forced to end its suzerain relationship with Korea. Korea is on its own, no longer a tributary state of China.

1905: The Russo-Japanese War ends in victory for Japan. Korea becomes a Japanese protectorate.

1907: After King Kojong fails to obtain international assistance to stop Japanese encroachments in Korea, he is forced to abdicate. Japan takes over Korea's internal administration.

1909: Prince Itō Hirobumi, the Japanese resident-general in Korea, is assassinated by a Korean, An Chunggun, in Harbin, Manchuria.

1910: The Korean government succumbs to Japanese pressure and signs a treaty of annexation on August 22. Korea becomes a colony of Japan.

1919: Former King Kojong dies. After nearly a decade of Japanese *budan seiji* (martial law rule), Koreans rise in spontaneous protest in what is called the March First Independence Movement.

1920: Japan shifts to a "cultural policy" (*bunka seiji*) in Korea, hoping to co-opt Korean support and diminish opposition.

1931: Japanese policy reverts to sterner rule under army generals. Throughout the 1930s Korea is used as a staging area for Japan's war across East Asia.

1945: The Allies defeat Japan and divide Korea into two occupation zones, north and south.

1948: Allied occupation forces turn their respective zones over to local governments, the Soviets to a socialist regime in the north, the Americans to a democratic capitalist regime in the south. Foreign armies pull back.

1950: The northern regime, led by Kim Il-sung, attempts to reunify the Korean Peninsula by military force. The Korean War ensues, with Chinese intervention in November.

1953: The Korean War ends in a cease-fire (armistice), roughly along the border where it started.

SOUTH KOREA

1960: The "Student Revolution" ends the rule of Syngman Rhee in South Korea. The democratic opposition experiments with a parliamentary government. Inflation and instability plague the South.

1961: In May, General Park Chung-hee emerges as military strongman following a coup d'état.

1963: South Korean army officers keep power after restoring constitutional rule and elections. The government launches a series of five-year economic plans.

1968: With South Korean forces supporting South Vietnam, North Korea steps up infiltration, espionage, and sabotage in a campaign to destabilize South Korea.

1979: President Park Chung-hee is assassinated. Army generals tighten their grip on power.

1987: Popular demonstrations force the military government to hold free elections. The democratic opposition splits, handing the presidency to another general.

1988: Seoul hosts the Summer Olympic Games.

1993: Kim Young-sam is inaugurated president, returning South Korea to civilian rule.

1997: South Korea suffers an economic crisis. The IMF intervenes with bailout funds and imposes fiscal discipline.

1998: Longtime democracy movement leader Kim Dae-jung becomes president of South Korea and announces the Sunshine Policy.

2000: Kim Dae-jung of South Korea and North Korean leader Kim Jong-il meet in Pyongyang.Kim Dae-jung is awarded the Nobel Peace Prize for his Sunshine Policy.

2002: South Korea and Japan co-host the FIFA World Cup soccer competition. South Korea makes the semifinals.

2008: Inauguration of former Seoul Mayor and longtime Hyundai corporation executive Lee Myung-bak as President; return to hard line policies toward North Korea.

2010: Amid tensions with North Korea, the sinking of the ROK Navy corvette *Cheonan*, presumably by a North Korean torpedo (March) and North Korean shelling of the ROK-held Yŏn'p'yŏng Island during a controversy over military maneuvers in a contested waters of the Yellow Sea off the west coast.

North Korea

1948: Soviet Union sponsors the creation of the Democratic People's Republic of Korea (DPRK) under the banner of the Korean Workers Party (the communist party) led by former Red Army major Kim Il-sung.

1950–53: The Korean War era. North Korea's cities and modern facilities are nearly destroyed by bombing.

1956: Kim Il-sung launches the Ch'ŏllima (Thousand-League Horse) Movement to boost industrial production in the DPRK, using the Kangsŏn Steel Works as a model.

1960: Kim Il-sung launches the Chŏngsanri Method campaign to boost agricultural production, using the village of Chŏngsanri as a model.

1961: The DPRK meets its targets in first five-year plan. Kim Il-sung is in an unchallengeable position.

1965: Kim Il-sung launches the Juche idea, meaning autonomy for the DPRK in politics, the economy, and national defense, seeking neutrality in the Sino-Soviet dispute.

1968: North Korea seizes a U.S. Navy intelligence ship and imprisons the crew, one of many incidents that include terrorist acts against South Korea and Japan over a period of years.

1970s: North Korea's economy, which initially outstripped the rate of growth in the South, begins to slow down.

1982 : Kim Jong-il authors the definitive text on the Juche idea as North Korea's governing ideology. He begins his long apprenticeship to become North Korea's leader.

1983: North Korean agents stage a terrorist attack in Burma, killing seventeen visiting South Korean officials and journalists.

1987: North Korean agents sabotage a Korean Air Lines passenger plane, killing 167 people over the Andaman Sea.

1991: North and South Korea are admitted separately as full members of the United Nations.

1993: North Korea withdraws from the Nuclear Non-Proliferation Treaty, protesting Western espionage and pressure.

1994: Kim Il-sung dies at the age of eighty-two.

1994: After a period of critical tension, the United States and DPRK sign an Agreed Framework by means of which the United States will organize financing of two light water reactors to produce electric power for the DPRK. North Korea which agrees to freeze its nuclear energy program.

1997: Experiencing a terrible famine, the DPRK summons its people to an Arduous March to sustain their society amid multiple disasters, including weather, floods, and the loss of socialist allies who no longer can aid North Korea.

1998: North Korea attempts to launch a communications satellite, sending a three-stage missile over Japanese territory to celebrate fifty years of the DPRK. Tensions rise in the region.

2000: The United States and North Korea tentatively agree on steps to end the DPRK's missile program. Secretary of State Madeline Albright visits Pyongyang and meets Chairman Kim Jong-il.

2002: President George W. Bush declares North Korea to be part of the Axis of Evil.

2003: The United States accuses North Korea of cheating on the Agreed Framework, ending it.

2003: With the United States, Russia, Japan, China, and South Korea, North Korea joins the Six Party Talks, aimed at negotiating ways to end the DPRK's nuclear program. Little progress is seen over the next several years.

2003-2010: Steady contraction of the North Korean economy.

2008: Chairman Kim Jong-il apparently suffers a stroke and a serious health crisis.

2009: Attempt to reissue new currency wipes out many illegal accumulations of private money and aggravates the ongoing financial crisis in the DPRK.

2010: Skirmishes with South Korea in disputed waters off the west coast of Korea. Kim Jong-il promotes his son, Kim Jong-un, and his sister, Kim Kyŏnghŭi to four-star general rank in the Korean People's Army, signaling the choice of Kim Jong-un as likely successor.

2011: Kim Jong-un appears in public with increasing frequency; Kim Jong-il appears to be recovering his health but in December suddenly dies from an apparent heart attack. The general population of the DPRK is thrown into mourning amid international speculation about the viability of Kim Jong-un as the new leader of the DPRK.

2012: Centennial of the birth of Kim Il-sung (1912–1994), founder of the DPRK, with the national goal of becoming a great power by his birthday on April 15.

CHINA

Mount Paektu

NORTH KOREA

•Sinuiju

East Sea

•Pyongyang

Inch'on• •Seoul

Yellow Sea

SOUTH KOREA

Kwangju

•Pusan

JAPAN

0 50 100 kilometers
0 50 100 miles

CHEJU

Map of the Korean Peninsula. Map courtesy of Diane Smith.

1

KOREA, THE UNITED STATES, AND THE WORLD

This book is about Korea and its people, their story, and why and how Korea is important to us. Readers in the United States are half a world away from Korea, but there are many things that tie the two countries and their peoples together. The United States fought a war in Korea in 1950–53; Korea and the United States have a military alliance and U.S. forces have been stationed in Korea for more than sixty years. Because of this, many Americans—millions actually—have personal experience in Korea. In recent years, Americans have visited, or lived in, Korea as tourists, educators, businesspeople, and missionaries. In the United States, many people are acquainted with Korean immigrants and Korean Americans. Americans buy Korean products from clothes to cars to electronics to kitchen appliances, and Korean brand names are household words: Hyundai, Samsung, and LG foremost among them. Many Americans enjoy Korean movies. American children go to Taekwondo classes after school. In New York, people buy food from Korean grocers. In south central Los Angeles, there is a "Koreatown" that looks so much like Seoul that Koreans actually think of it as an extension of their capital. And every major American city has not one but several Korean churches that serve as hubs for Korean residents. Clearly, the two countries have a lot invested in each other.

Korea is a "key issue" in Asian studies mainly because of its recent political history and economic success but also because of its longevity as a culture. On the world map it seems small and vulnerable. However, the people of Korea have maintained their unique civilization through many centuries, relying on their resilience and shared characteristics. The most important of these is the Korean language, which is separate from Chinese and Japanese. It is the foundation of a national culture that includes a social system based on Confucian ethics and many influences from China,

1

in particular, but also a distinctive array of Korean lifeways that include local religions; Korean cuisine; folk arts, including literature and music; and a fierce determination to repel domination from the outside. Korean culture is shared by a significant number of people—more than 72 million Koreans, most of them in their homeland but a considerable number in expatriate communities around the world.

If Korea seems small on the map, by other measures it is a significant world civilization. In terms of population, for example, the Korean Peninsula outranks a number of better-known countries in the West, including Great Britain, France, Spain, and the other countries of Western Europe with the exception of the reunited Germany. In terms of economic output, the Republic of Korea, or "South Korea," ranks fifteenth in the world, in a group with Australia and Mexico, and ahead of many advanced societies such as the Netherlands and Sweden. In terms of world sports, South Korea is a major player in the Olympics and FIFA World Cup, as well as the Asian Games, and Korean golfers are top contenders in tournaments around the world. And in the world of film, Korean directors such as Im Kwŏntaek and Park Chan-wook are internationally respected for their cinematography.

KOREAN AMERICANS: THE KOREANS WE KNOW BEST

The world also knows Korea through the many Koreans who have migrated abroad and comprise what scholars sometimes call the "Korean diaspora." In addition to the 48.6 million people in South Korea and the 22.7 million in North Korea that are reported in the 2010 CIA World Fact Book, there are an estimated 2 million ethnic Koreans in China (mostly in southern Manchuria just over the Korean border), 1.4 million in the United States, 600,000 in Japan, 300,000 in Central Asia (mainly Uzbekistan and Kazakhstan), about 125,000 in Russia (mainly on Sakhalin Island and the Primorsk region close to Vladivostok), 125,000 in Brazil, 110,000 in Canada, and smaller numbers in various countries of Southeast Asia, Latin America, and Europe.[1]

Most of these people are in various stages of assimilation, adjusting to life in their adopted countries. In Central Asia, the Koreans who call themselves "Koryŏ-saram" (People of Koryŏ) were forcibly sent there by the Soviet government in the 1930s to get them out of the Primorsk region, where they were thought to comprise a worrisome, and possibly disloyal, population. After many decades in the republics of Central Asia, many Koryŏ-saram have intermarried with local people, and their children know almost nothing about Korea. Modern history saw a number of forced relocations of Koreans, including workers who were drafted by imperial Japan to work on Sakhalin Island, north of Japan, and in the mines and factories of Japan itself, during the decades of Japanese colonial rule over Korea, 1910–45. Descendants of Koreans on Sakhalin and in Japan suffer many disadvantages because of their ethnic identity and minority status. In Japan, for example, although it is possible for Koreans to become naturalized citizens, most retain their identities as "Chōsenjin" (People of Chōsen) and are permanent residents, not citizens, meaning that they cannot vote and therefore have no way to participate in the Japanese political system.

Korean Americans also have a history that relates to events in the twentieth century. Although their stories likewise vary by individuals, their migration to America happened in several waves and patterns. At the beginning of the 1900s, labor contractors from Hawaii recruited Korean workers to help farm the cane fields just after Hawaii became a U.S. territory. When they sent for "picture brides" from back home, they started families, which became the foundation of the large Korean community in Hawaii.[2]

Over the next several decades, a trickle of Koreans from Hawaii founded the Korean communities in California and on the East Coast, mainly in Washington, D.C. American officials were often puzzled about their identity, since they insisted that they were not Japanese, yet they had originated in what the United States then recognized as part of the Japanese empire. Some of their leaders tried to organize resistance movements to win American support for efforts to throw the Japanese out of their homeland. These efforts were not successful, and between 1910 and 1945 the Koreans in America slowly "Americanized" themselves, buying farms and small businesses, organizing associations, having children who were American citizens by birth, and sending the children to schools where they often acquired advanced educations and pursued significant careers. During World War Two, quite a few Korean American men served in the U.S. Armed Forces, and some of them got their chance to fight against Japan.

The first generations of Korean Americans suffered racial discrimination, and most old-time Korean American families can tell stories about how they were denied housing and access to services just because they looked Asian. Because of discrimination, and because their numbers were few, they tended to concentrate in tight communities often organized around churches. Churches, then as now, have always served as community centers for Korean Americans, helping newcomers find jobs and teaching them how to solve the myriad problems of adjusting to life in a new country. Older newcomers, especially, had a hard time learning English well enough to function on their own, and the churches and Korean small businesses that employed them enabled them to lessen the pain of their isolation by speaking their own language and being part of a relatively familiar Korean social system.[3]

When Japan was driven from Korea by the Allied victory in 1945, and especially in the Korean War years (1950–53) and until 1965, new trends and opportunities brought many more Koreans to the United States. American colleges, especially church-related colleges connected to missionary organizations in Korea, welcomed Korean students who knew enough English to survive and could pay tuition and offered scholarships to bright Koreans who otherwise could not have come. Among the many thousands of soldiers who served in Korea, there were some who fell in love with Korean girls and brought them home as "war brides." In 1955, an Oregon farmer named Harry Holt got approval to adopt eight Korean children fathered by American servicemen, beginning a new avenue of Korean American assimilation through adoption.

Korean scholarship students, war brides, and adoptees occupy special positions in the history of immigration to the United States because they did not have the Korean support systems that normally served the immigrant community. Their isolation also varied with the individual. Korean college students often faced personal crises when they graduated and were legally obliged to go home but wanted to stay or when they tried to date Americans and ran into racial barriers. War brides often adjusted well to their new families but in many cases were overwhelmed by having to adapt, learn new customs and manners, and deal with many new relatives, not all of whom were as accepting as their soldier husbands. Divorces were not uncommon, and ex-brides usually were at a tremendous disadvantage to make a living. Other Korean immigrants in the United States tended to look down on them, and their own families back in Korea discouraged them from returning and advised them to stay in America where their chances were altogether better. There were many variations in the adoption process as well. Many adoptees report that they thought they were as "white" as their siblings and parents until they became aware of their difference in the "tween" or teen years, often undergoing painful identity crises.

In 1965, the United States altered its immigration laws to permit families to enter the United States and seek citizenship. At the time, Korea was still suffering from the devastation of the Korean War. Many people in South Korea regarded the United States as a paradise that offered jobs, education for their children, and opportunities for every kind of advancement. In addition, there were many former North Korean refugees in South Korea for whom life had been exceedingly hard since their departure from their original homes in the north. They also sought immigration status in the United States, where it seemed the effort to start over would be much more fruitful.

Thus the U.S. Immigration and Nationality Act of 1965, informally known as the "Brothers and Sisters Act," brought rapid growth and change to Korean American communities all across the country. The new law enabled Korean immigrants in the United States to act as financial guarantors and sponsors for relatives who were seeking to follow them to America. Korean communities suddenly became highly visible. An area called "Koreatown" spread over many blocks of south central Los Angeles. Korean communities also grew in Queens, New York, and northern New Jersey, in Chicago, and in other major cities. In Los Angeles, which is known as "Nasŏng" in Korean, people started referring to Koreatown as "Nasŏng-gu," a detached borough, or "gu," of Seoul.[4]

Figure 1.1: Koreatown, Los Angeles. Photo by Donald Clark.

The burgeoning of Korean communities in America has brought serious friction, most dramatically demonstrated by the Los Angeles riots of 1992, when the largely African American population erupted into violence and vandalism against Korean merchants who were seen as living off the neighborhood while moving themselves to comfortable suburbs with the profits from their downtown shops. This outbreak was a wake-up call for Korean immigrants that led to elaborate efforts to improve community relations. Koreans in America learned that they had to realign their own thinking, to reach outside their own ethnic circles to become full participants in American life.

The life patterns of Korean immigrants can include dramatic downward mobility for the first generation of newcomers. It is hard work, and personally traumatic, to move from a familiar country and culture into an entirely new system where everyone is already established. Immigrants are not visitors: they intend to sink roots and stay. So the people who migrated from South Korea to the United States, with high expectations and much anxiety, were often disappointed and disillusioned by what they found. Medical doctors found that their English skills were not good enough to get licenses to practice medicine. Teachers, engineers, and other professionals were stymied, either by the language barrier or the lack of capital to get started, just to cite a couple of the problems. Many highly educated Koreans found themselves running grocery stands and liquor stores and tailor shops, just to survive. Their social lives revolved around the Korean churches that sprang up in the neighborhoods where they lived and in little strip malls comprised of Korean-owned businesses. Working long hours and scrimping and saving, they put enough money away to send their children to college, often to colleges in the Ivy League. Such are the best success stories in the history of the Korean American population.

Success stories are part of the picture, but with Korean Americans numbering nearly 1.5 million and their dispersal in every state and city in the United States, circumstances now vary widely. Some immigrants go back to Korea after retirement, still drawing U.S. Social Security checks, keeping in daily contact with their children in America, and marveling at what Korea has become in their absence. The children of many Korean immigrants are completely immersed in their professions and no longer identify much with Korea, the ancestral homeland that has receded one or two generations into their families' past. There are generational conflicts, for example, between immigrant parents, who want to keep some of the old values of Korea, and their children, who seem to be more interested

6

in social networking with their friends and following American sports, music, and television.

As life has improved in South Korea, there is less and less "push" for Korean immigration to America. As communications and transportation have made the world smaller, and Seoul just a thirteen-hour nonstop hop from Los Angeles, there is even less reason for families to use immigration as a way to stay together. As a result, we now see Korean immigration as less of a wave and more of an individual choice, made with better information and more realistic expectations about what awaits on the other side of the Pacific.

THE KOREA THAT WE KNOW

Geography is one key to understanding Korean history. The fact that it is a peninsula has helped it stay isolated. The seas around Korea limit expansion, but they also protect Korea from the kinds of warfare that swept across the contiguous boundaries of Europe. On the other hand, unlike Europeans, the people of Korea did not strike out across the oceans

Figure 1.2: Hillside tea plantation, South Chŏlla Province. Photo by Donald Clark.

to explore or spread their religion or seek dominion over colonies abroad. Compared to Spain, Portugal, Holland, and England, Korea would appear to have been inward oriented, concerned mainly with its own business. When there was contact with China or Japan on either side, or with the tribal societies of Manchuria to the north, the Koreans quickly sensed their limitations. This went both ways: while Koreans couldn't expand, they also fiercely defended their peninsula from outside encroachment. On the other hand, there was continual contact with border peoples to the north, and notable cultural and trade links, as during the Silla period when Korea communicated with China and Central Asia via the Silk Road. Korea was vaguely known in the Arab world because of this traffic, existing as a distant and mysterious land rumored to be rich in gold.[5]

The Korean Peninsula is resource poor in some ways but resource rich in others. Korea is rich in minerals, for example, and forests in the north, as well as abundant water resources. The surrounding sea is a rich source of protein in the Korean diet. However, mountains are the dominant feature of the Korean landscape, limiting the amount of arable land. This is especially true in the north, where a short growing season is the result of a combination of latitude and altitude. North Korea in fact has only a strip along the east coast and a limited amount of level land in the west on which to grow grain. South Korea is different: the valleys are broader, and food sufficiency is the modern norm. The surrounding seas are a source of abundant protein. So, when Korea had a primarily agricultural economy, its people lived essentially on subsistence agriculture. Although Koreans supported themselves, they barely had a surplus of anything, and masses of common people lived in wretched poverty.

Modern times have altered the relationship between Korea's land and people and their ability to live well. In the early twentieth century, when Korea started industrializing, factories and power plants were concentrated in the north, where the resource base was better for modern industry. In the latter half of the twentieth century, the fertile terrain of southern Korea, while supporting a population twice as large as that in the north, managed, with good policy planning and considerable foreign aid, to lift itself out of poverty. Then, following an economic strategy based on export-led industrialization, South Korea's hardworking people created for themselves an almost undreamed of standard of living by the year 2000. In contrast, North Korea, suffering from harsher weather and tougher terrain, food shortages, the failures of socialist economics, and isolation from the world trading system, continues in poverty.

The energy sector is a good example of the contrast between the two systems. South Korea is completely integrated with the world energy system, importing 95 percent of its petroleum and other energy needs and generating much of its electricity in nuclear plants. North Korea, cut off from energy subsidies that it enjoyed before the fall of the Soviet Union, has been thrown into a long-term energy crisis. This, too, can be seen as a North Korean failure, but it is also because the international system, led by the United States, has regarded North Korea as a dangerous threat, a violator of international norms, and therefore deserving of economic and political sanctions. North Korea's resort to developing its abundant supplies of natural uranium into nuclear power has not helped the situation. Uranium can also be used to make weapons that would make North Korea a mortal danger to its neighbors. The outside world, led by the United States, has done everything possible to keep North Korea from acquiring nuclear power, not only trying to prevent it from becoming a nuclear military power but also preventing its using nuclear fuel to ameliorate its energy crisis, as has been done by all its neighbors, including South Korea, which runs as many as eighteen nuclear plants to power its thoroughly modern economy.

In the world media, news about Korea today typically represents one of two different story lines: Korea the trouble spot and Korea the economic "miracle." The first comes from the fact that Korea at present is divided, North and South, into two mutually hostile nation-states, offering moments of conflict and crisis that make for sensational headlines in the world press. The second comes from the efforts of the Korean people themselves, notably South Korea's remarkable economic growth, advanced technology, prominence in world trade, and achievement of democratic reforms. It is the "trouble" headlines that seem to leave the deeper impression in the West. The second narrative, although it represents much more in terms of human achievement and real success, usually gets less attention.

South Korea's economic surge since 1980 certainly has revolutionized the way the international community regards the Korean people and what their country means to the world. *Miracle* is the word often used to describe the transformation of South Korea from a broken agricultural country, one of the poorest in the world, to membership in the front ranks of the world's developed nations in less than half a century. But *miracle* is not appropriate to describe the hard work and sacrifice that the people of South Korea poured into their country's future. It is not an exaggeration to say that between 1960 and 1990 two generations of Korean adults, in striving for a better future for their children, shouldered incredibly heavy burdens, worked brutal hours, took serious personal risks, underwent wrenching relocations from farms to cities, and endured long years of intimidation under military dictatorship, all without any assurance that they would succeed. Since 1990 Korea has also had to weather market uncertainties that have made it tricky to consolidate the gains laid on the foundation of those two earlier generations. But altogether it is through the efforts of the Korean people themselves—not because of any miracle—that their country has become a modern, urban, industrial democracy. That re-creation is the biggest story in the history of modern Korea and is a major topic of chapter 4.

This achievement is regularly noted by a major constituency of Americans who are personally connected to Korea through military service. The United Nations soldiers, mostly Americans, who fought in the Korean War (1950–53) and spent time stationed in bases on the Korean Peninsula for decades thereafter, generally remember Korea as a muddy, boring, and mostly hopeless place—impressions exaggerated, no doubt, by military base life. The South Korean government likes to organize reunion tours for former soldiers to show them what Korea has become. Among the qualities that most strike the returnees are the cleanliness (compared to the muddy country they remember), and the electric energy that lights the cities, runs the bullet trains, and powers the giant advertising screens in downtown Seoul. They note that people are well dressed, own cars, and live in surprisingly comfortable apartment complexes. The government tries to show the visitors that their service in more difficult times was a basic element in the success of South Korea as a healthy democracy and prosperous economy and that the lives of the many United Nations soldiers who died in the Korean War were not sacrificed in vain.

Americans and Koreans therefore have had quite a lot to do with each other over a long period of time. Millions of lives have intersected in the relations between the people of the United States and South, and even North, Korea. On many levels it is remarkable that Koreans and Americans know each other as well as they do. The Korean Peninsula, after all, is far away and easy to overlook. But we need to know more than just the news, the cars, and the stories of soldiers and immigrants. In the following chapters, the subject is Korea itself: what it looks like, what the Korean people have been through, and what may be awaiting them—and us—in the twenty-first century.

2

THE KOREAN PEOPLE

THEIR LAND AND THEIR STORY

The Korean Peninsula is approximately the size of the state of Minnesota. However, unlike Minnesota, Korea is covered with steep mountains and jagged peaks. The people live among the mountains in valleys and hillsides and along rivers and streams. A famous Korean saying goes, "Over the mountain are more mountains." Compared to the American Rockies or the Himalayas, Korean mountains are not particularly high. Most rise to no more than four thousand feet, and they make for ideal hiking. But they make it hard to travel far from home. Until very recently, therefore, most Koreans spent their whole lives on farms near the place where they were born. Today, even in modern Seoul, for example, nearly everyone is only one or two generations away from farm life. Either they or their parents have had the experience of moving from farm to city. Accordingly, the memory of their home region is strong and they continue to identify with particular places outside of the capital region, where nearly half of all South Koreans now live.

Thus the people of Korea are very conscious of different areas within the country and identify strongly with the place where their families started out. Koreans often show their regional roots in the way they speak. While there is a "standard" way of pronouncing Korean—"standard Korean" is what is heard on the radio and television—there are still regional dialects. The differences are quite noticeable between the Korean spoken in South Korea, for example, and that spoken in the North. And within South Korea there are speech patterns that set Cheju Island apart, for example, and others that make it possible to tell whether someone is from the southeast or southwest.

Foods and flavors also distinguish Korea's regions, with Pyongyang in the North famous for its buckwheat noodles (*naengmyŏn*) and Seoul

11

known for its elegant dishes derived from royal kitchens. A signature Seoul dish is *sinsŏllo*, which consists of thin slices of beef in broth cooked in a brass brazier on the table. Southeastern Korea has abundant seafood and is famous for *p'ajŏn*, a pancake made from batter that contains clams and shrimp. The southwest is known for especially hot *kimch'i* and the working-class lunch favorite *pibimpap,* a mélange of vegetables, rice, eggs, and sometimes ground meat. The city of Taejŏn is known for an ox-bone soup called *sŏlŏngtang.* Taegu is known for apples. Cheju Island is famous for oranges and bananas.[1]

These variations help make Korea interesting, and they also foster stereotypes and historical grievances. In recent decades, for example, South Korean politics has been largely dominated by leaders from the southeast, and in at least one election—the election of 1997, which made Kim Dae-Jung president—regional voting patterns were crucial. It might seem odd to an outsider to see how much difference regional affiliations make to Koreans in a country that is so small. However, it goes far beyond speech patterns and food. Indeed, it is difficult to comprehend the virulence of the division between North and South Korea, for example, or the shape of modern politics in South Korea, without first recognizing the power of regional identification.

KOREAN BEGINNINGS

Historians differ over when "Korea" actually became a "nation" in the way we understand the term. The two republics on the Korean Peninsula actually date back only to 1948. The kingdoms that ruled over most parts of Korea before 1900 did not always control all of it. But the ancient Chinese thought of Korea as a civilization, certainly, and they gave it a name, Ch'ao-hsien (or Chaoxian), the "Land of the Morning Calm," which suggests a place with people carrying on their particular way of life. Ch'ao-hsien, or Chosŏn in Korean, always considered itself a local community, and no matter which kingdom was ruling over which territory on the peninsula, for centuries the ancestors of today's Koreans fought off encroachments from the tribes to the north, the Chinese to the west, and the Japanese to the east.

However, Korea's position between China and Japan also meant that the ancestors of the Koreans had to find ways to relate to, and in some cases accommodate, their stronger neighbors. With notable exceptions—such as the Mongol and Manchu invasions and the war with Japan in the 1590s—most of the time Korea has managed to maintain its independence.

12

This is even true since the division of Korea by the Allies in 1945, after which, for the most part, the two rival states in the north and south have been autonomous.

According to Korea's main creation legend, the earth was made in misty antiquity by a deity named Hwan'in. The creator's son, named Hwan'ung, descended to live on the earth, on Mount Paektu (Paektu-san), in what is now Korea. However, with forest animals as his only companions, he was lonely. One day a tiger and a bear asked Hwan'ung to transform them into people. Hwan'ung proposed a contest: the tiger and the bear would go into a cave with a supply of wild roots for food, and whichever one could last a hundred days and nights in the cave would be turned into a human being. The tiger by nature was too impatient to last the hundred days, but the bear, being used to hibernating, stayed in the whole time and emerged to be transformed into a beautiful woman. Hwan'ung married her, and their first child was a son named Tan'gun.

When Tan'gun grew up he inherited his father's kingdom, which he moved to what is now the area of Pyongyang, the capital of what is now North Korea. There he founded the state of Chosŏn, whose people were the ancestors of today's Koreans.[2]

The Tan'gun story, Mount Paektu, the mountain animals, the name Chosŏn, and the city of Pyongyang are all reminders of Korea's beloved foundation story. Indeed, in the 1990s, North Korean archaeologists discovered the location of what they assert to be Tan'gun's tomb on the outskirts of Pyongyang in the 1990s. The government built a magnificent mausoleum there to honor Tan'gun's memory.

Koreans are entitled to their creation story, but historians have to rely on other kinds of evidence for clues about the distant past. Archaeological studies of stones and tool fragments suggest that the earliest ancestors of the Korean people migrated southward into the peninsula from Central Asia and Siberia over the course of many generations. This idea is reinforced by the existence of stone tomb structures called "dolmens," which are found across northern Eurasia all the way west to Finland. Excavations indicate that the early inhabitants of the peninsula lived in pit dwellings and made vessels out of clay for storing food, decorating their pots with "comb markings." Fragments of weapons suggest that they hunted and fished for meat, which they cooked over open fires.[3]

To do this, they would have had to work together in teams, suggesting that they lived in organized communities under some form of authority, whether familial or tribal. Their lives developed, perhaps with influence from the area that is now China, and they started using metal, notably bronze, to make knives, weapons, tools, and containers. These things resemble similar items found in North China, presenting evidence that people from China were also moving in to live among the earliest Koreans. By the first millennium BCE we see signs that the Korean Peninsula was part of a much larger regional way of life that involved settlements and shared patterns of social organization, religion, agriculture, hunting, fishing, and warfare.

THE SHAPE OF KOREAN HISTORY

Korea's earliest communities were tribal confederations that occupied the territory in the northern part of the peninsula and beyond, into land that is now part of China. Some of these tribal states were under Chinese rule at different times, and in 108 BCE China's Han dynasty (206 BCE–220 CE) established a base at Pyongyang, making it the center of a colony called Lolang (Korean: Nangnang). By the time Lolang disappeared, around 300 CE, the Korean people had created three kingdoms of their own: Koguryŏ in the north, Paekche in the southwest, and Silla in the southeast.

THE THREE KINGDOMS PERIOD

Koguryŏ was the oldest and strongest of Korea's Three Kingdoms. Its civilization was based on hunting, and its men were skilled warriors. The people of Koguryŏ were descended from the earlier Puyŏ (Chinese: Fu-yü) people of central Manchuria, who had moved south into the Korean Peninsula, dislodging the Chinese colonies and developing their own nation. A high point of Koguryŏ history came under King Kwanggaet'o (391–413), whose expansion campaigns extended Koguryŏ power in all directions. A stone stele that was discovered early in the twentieth century on the northern bank of the Yalu River attests to the exploits of King Kwanggaet'o as his men pushed northward into the Manchurian Plain.

Koguryŏ's military blocked several attempts by Chinese armies to reassert their presence on the Korean Peninsula. As Koguryŏ matured, however, it also learned many things from China. Buddhism, Confucianism, law, taxation, and administration are some of the things that Koguryŏ imported and adapted. The style and art of royal tombs in the Pyongyang area demonstrate Koguryŏ's adaptation of Chinese symbols of kingship and aristocracy.

Figure 2.1: Ch'ŏnji, the "Lake of Heaven," atop Mount Paektu. Photo courtesy of Eckart Dege.

In the southwest, a smaller kingdom called Paekche started out by breaking away from Koguryŏ. First located near today's city of Seoul, on the Han River, it was forced by Koguryŏ to move farther south, where ultimately it was defeated in the year 660. Paekche ruins suggest a refined style marked by tombs and earthworks in the Seoul area and Buddhist temple remains and royal tumuli at its later capitals of Kongju and Puyŏ farther south. Paekche carried on trade with the islands of Japan, and today some of the most beautiful examples of Paekche Buddhist art and architecture are to be found in Japan, where Korean artisans shared their skills with Japanese apprentices.[4]

Silla made good use of Chinese help to defeat Paekche in 660, and Koguryŏ in 668, creating the first unified Korean state. But even though beholden to the Chinese forces that were sent by the Tang dynastic court, Silla refused to submit to Chinese overlordship and did not become a colony. Instead, Silla and Tang worked out an arrangement whereby Korea would be China's "little brother," pledging to be a submissive neighbor while enjoying Chinese protection. Silla promised never to join in alliances with China's enemies, and China promised to let the Koreans rule themselves within their own territory. This became the pattern for "tributary relations," which involved periodic embassies to China to offer tribute to the emperor and to renew the pledge of Korea's continued submission.

The bond between emperor and king helped the Korean monarch hold power because it would have been very hard to challenge someone who was approved by the emperor. This pattern of tributary relations continued through many centuries until 1895, when it finally broke down.

The old Silla capital at Kyŏngju contains many relics and monuments that tell of the advance of Korean civilization between the fifth and tenth centuries.[5] The royal tombs of Silla show Korea's debt to Tang China as the kingdom organized its life as a nation headed by a *wang* (王), or "king," whose title associated him with Chinese-style ruling. Silla made Buddhism the state religion, constructing elaborate temples that connected the king with religious authority. Silla borrowed Chinese ideas of administration, creating a government of specialized offices that performed government functions such as taxation, defense, and justice more efficiently. Silla traders amassed fortunes carrying goods back and forth to China. Silla monks made pilgrimages to China and even India to study Buddhism. Silla scholars studied government in the Tang capital of Chang'an. In these ways, Silla further integrated the civilization of the Korean Peninsula with the shared higher culture of East Asia.

However, it was also natural for Korea to retain uniquely Korean things. The Korean social structure continued to be defined by clans, with aristocratic families in castes, called "bone ranks," starting with the royal caste, or sacred bone, and working down to commoners in hereditary occupations and even slaves. Silla warriors organized themselves into guards called the *hwarang*, young men who excelled at martial arts while also cultivating knowledge of literature and an appreciation of nature.

Silla succeeded in extending its sway over most of the Korean Peninsula in 668 CE, and the ensuing "United Silla" period lasted until 935. Today, the ancient capital of Kyŏngju remains "a museum without walls," with Silla tombs, monuments, temples, and even bits of palaces in neighborhoods throughout the valley. The city's museum displays golden crowns, jewelry, gems, documents, and other artifacts, such as clothing and weapons, that show the beauty and refinement of Silla culture. The greatest Silla artifacts are Pulguk-sa (Temple of Buddhaland) and the Sŏkkuram grotto, a stone cave on a nearby mountainside, which houses a majestic Buddha image that overlooks the eastern sea in the distance.

By the 800s, the social and political system of Silla was having trouble maintaining itself as a nation. Burdened by taxes and confined by social regulations, angry people raised rebellions. A king had been assassinated in the year 780. Rich families were removing their lands from the government tax rolls. To the southwest there was a revival of the ancient state of Paekche. In the north there rose "Later Koguryŏ." In 918 a nobleman named Wang Gŏn seized control of the Koguryŏ territory, changed its name to Koryŏ, and set out to unify the peninsula by defeating Silla and then Paekche, a task that was completed by the year 936.

MEDIEVAL KOREA: THE KINGDOM OF KORYO, 918–1392

Korea gets its English name from "Koryŏ," which is the old "Koguryŏ" kingdom name without the middle syllable. Around the world, Koryŏ is best remembered for its celadon pottery, a style of graceful bowls, vases, pitchers, and other objects that were covered with painted and incised designs and then covered with "celadon glaze," a glaze of a subtle gray-green color, which Koryŏ potters perfected in the twelfth century.

Within Korea, however, the Koryŏ period represents a transition from the tribal and clan-centered style of social and political organization that was typical of Silla at its height and the centralized national system that became typical of traditional Korea until modern times. The shift began when Wang Gŏn set up a capital with a royal court supported by a government bureaucracy in a new city, Kaesŏng, in west-central Korea. This location made it much easier to control (and tax) the entire peninsula.

By the year 1000, the Koryŏ capital at Kaesŏng had a central bureaucracy whose members were chosen by examination in a selection system adopted from China. The examination system was designed to pick qualified leaders based on their education and mastery of the Chinese classics, a series of texts that stressed moral behavior and historical and literary knowledge.

Highly qualified leaders made the Koryŏ state much stronger than Silla had been, and the dynasty moved to expand its frontiers in order to recover lost territory to the north. This created conflict with the Khitan people in the nearby Liao Peninsula. There were three successive wars with the Khitans, and in the years 993 and 1010 the Khitans invaded far enough into Koryŏ to attack the capital city of Kaesŏng. The Koreans managed to repel the third Khitan invasion in 1018 and followed that by building a physical wall from the mouth of the Yalu River southeast across the whole peninsula to the eastern shore just north of modern Wŏnsan.

It was Koryŏ's fate to be forced to defend against invaders during most of its history. Following the Khitans came the Jurchen nomads from the forests of Manchuria, a federation of tribes so powerful that they were able to crush the Khitans, first, and then to invade China proper, establishing themselves on the site of modern Beijing and forcing the Chinese Song dynasty to retreat south of the Yangzi River. Indeed, the Jurchens, who set up a dynasty that they called the "Jin," which lasted in China from 1127 to 1234, dealt China one of the worst defeats recorded in its entire history.

The wars with the Khitans shifted Korean tributary payments away from China. The Jurchens in turn did not overrun Korea, but they did force Koryŏ to transfer tributary loyalty to their "empire." In this way, Koryŏ managed to use the payment of tribute, first to the Khitans and then to the Jurchens, to purchase safety from even worse disasters. This was, of course, humiliating. The tributary system devised between Silla and the Tang had honored the cultural power and supremacy of China, which was acknowledged as a unique center of civilization. But when it came to submitting tribute to barbarians like the Khitans and Jurchens, Koreans resented having to admit their weakness before more warlike neighbors.

In the year 958, the kingdom of Koryŏ began using the Chinese-style examination system to test the qualifications of its candidates for office, but it took many years for this system to replace older patterns of appointment. In the meantime, the king's relatives and personal supporters kept their grip on wealth and power. These privileged characters were paid with grants of land and slaves. They lived in the capital and collected large rents from the people who worked their lands in the provinces. Certain court favorites became very wealthy living off the labor of slaves and poor farmers, who had to pay rent for the use of their land. In fact it remained more important to be related to someone powerful than to seek advancement on one's own merits through education and the state examinations.

The system of granting "salary lands" to noblemen in the government assumed that when they died the government would take the land back and assign it to someone else. However, the nobles invented ways to pass their salary lands to their heirs when they died, making for accumulations of land in the hands of families that got richer and richer. The nobles typically paid no tax on their accumulated estates, which were called *nongjang*, and as the *nongjang* grew they took considerable amounts of land off the tax rolls, creating a fiscal problem. The government was forced to make common people pay higher taxes just to make up the difference. Some commoners had such a hard time paying their taxes that they actually volunteered to give themselves and their lands to the noblemen because it was easier to be a slave on a *nongjang* estate than to be a free person who had to pay taxes.

Officials and *nongjang* owners were only the top layer of Koryŏ society. Most Koreans were commoners, and most commoners were small farmers. In theory, farmers were honorable because they produced food, which was basic to life. In fact, however, small farmers were marks for government officials, who drove them mercilessly to increase production and pay more taxes. Farmers' lives, therefore, were miserable. Farm children rarely received any education and thus were doomed to work in the fields for their entire lives. Even worse were the lives of those lower on the social scale—not only slaves but also *ch'ŏnmin*, or "base people," people with the least desirable jobs in the system such as miners, woodcutters, and, lowest of all, handlers of meat, leather, and the dead. There was very little chance to move upward in this social system. Without family wealth, a Korean young person could hardly afford an education or expect to become something better than his or her parents.

At the upper end of the social scale, the aristocracy, especially in the capital city of Kaesŏng, lived a very different life. Koryŏ culture was strongly Buddhist, and temples and monasteries were richly supported by the Korean upper class, whose donations were meant as acts of piety to win favor with the Buddha. Being wealthy, the temples became centers of culture and intellectual life. Temples used their wealth to commission valuable works of religious art, including paintings and images of Buddhist deities. These valuable objects meant training some of the monks to be guards and defenders, beginning Korea's tradition of martial arts, which is best known today for Taekwŏndo. Some devout Buddhist commoners solved their tax problems by giving their lands to the temples, enriching the temples while they enjoyed a certain security working the land as "temple slaves."

Buddhist ideas spread quickly during the Koryŏ period and reflect much of the diversity in the world of Buddhist tradition. In Korea, however, they clustered along two main lines. One was the "pietistic" line, which stressed the weakness and unworthiness of the believer, who would cast himself before the Buddha in a plea for mercy, in effect seeking "salvation." Praying for salvation and performing acts of piety were characteristics of this type.

The other strain is referred to as the "meditative" type, often associated with Zen Buddhism (the better-known Japanese term for what Koreans call Sŏn and Chinese call Chan). Zen Buddhists believed that salvation, or "enlightenment," could be found within, and they struggled to clear their minds of distractions and find salvation through meditation or intuition.

Spirited debates took place between leaders of these two currents of Koryŏ Buddhism. Meanwhile the entire nation piously sought the blessing and protection of the Buddha. In the midst of the Khitan wars, the government committed itself to a supreme act of religious devotion: the publication of the entire text of the sermons, laws, and commentaries that together comprise the Buddhist canon, or *Tripitaka*. Hundreds of scribes and woodcarvers created the printing blocks necessary to publish the quarter million pages of the *Tripitaka*. On uniform planks of cured wood they spent years carving, in reverse, enough columns of Chinese characters to put four pages of the *Tripitaka* on each wooden block, two to a side, until they had carved more than eighty-one thousand blocks. A few precious copies were then printed by inking the blocks and pressing sheets of fine paper onto them, creating pages of printed text that were bound into books and lovingly studied by the worthiest scholars. At the time, the *Tripitaka Koreana* was one of the greatest achievements of Korean civilization.

Koryŏ, meanwhile, developed in many other areas. In 1145 the scholar Kim Pusik produced his history of Korea up to that point, the earliest written history that still exists, entitled *Samguk Sagi*, or "History of the

Figure 2.2: Rows of wooden printing blocks for the *Tripitaka Koreana* stored at Hae'insa Temple. Photo by Donald Clark.

Three Kingdoms." Chinese potters, fleeing unrest and fighting in China, arrived on Korea's coasts and set up kilns, teaching Koryŏ potters how to make what evolved into the famous Koryŏ celadon, the best-known Korean contribution to the world of ceramic art.

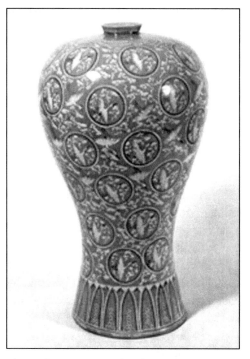

Figure 2.3: An example of Koryŏ celadon.

In Kaesŏng during the 1100s, more powerful stresses developed within the Koryŏ aristocracy, expressed in uprisings that culminated in a military coup d'état by a general named Ch'oe Ch'unghŏn, in 1196. A main reason for Ch'oe's coup was long-running discrimination by civilians against the military. Although Koryŏ needed soldiers for defense, they were far down the social pecking order and their officers were never accepted as full members of the capital nobility no matter what their rank or accomplishments. Ch'oe's coup used the anger of the military class to take control of the court in Kaesŏng and to rule in the manner of a Japanese shogun, using the king as a puppet. He and his heirs ruled Koryŏ for nearly thirty years, weakening and corrupting the country's political system while keeping kings on the throne as tools.[6]

In the early 1200s the Mongols rose to become a mighty force that scourged the length and breadth of the Eurasian continent. In 1231 the Mongols invaded Korea, burning and looting villages as they went and even destroying the sacred printing blocks for the Buddhist *Tripitaka*. When they captured Kaesŏng and forced the court to surrender, the Ch'oe military dictators tried to carry on resistance. However, when an assassin put an end to the last Ch'oe dictator, the Koryŏ king surrendered to the Mongols, agreeing to pay tribute.

Mongol overlordship was worse for Koryŏ than anything that had gone before. The Mongols took Korean princes hostage and raised and educated them in their capital at Tat'u (Beijing), even forcing them to marry Mongol women. As Korean princes and princesses married Mongols, the blood lines of successive generations of Koryŏ royalty became less and less Korean. The Mongols also maintained certain Korean princes as possible substitutes, ready to replace the reigning monarch in Kaesŏng if he ever misbehaved. The Mongols put military forces in Korea, creating a kind of occupation. For their two attempted invasions of Japan in 1279 and 1284, they drafted Koreans as soldiers and forced others to harvest lumber from Korean hills and build their invasion fleets.

After being reduced to the status of a Mongol provincial government, the state of Koryŏ was in no position to survive the collapse of the greater Mongol empire in the middle of the fourteenth century. Internally weakened by corruption, quarrels among factions of the nobility, ruination of the tax and land systems, and decades of humiliation by the Mongols, the government was readily overthrown by military challengers in the 1380s. One of these, a general named Yi Sŏnggye, took control with the backing of a reform faction and established a new dynasty and government in 1392.

EARLY CHOSON, 1392–1600

The Korean kingdom founded by General Yi Sŏnggye resumed using the ancient name of Chosŏn, although the period is sometimes also referred to as the Yi dynasty. A total of twenty-seven kings from the Yi clan of Chŏnju, all descendants of Yi Sŏnggye, reigned in Chosŏn between 1392 and 1910, an unusually long time for a kingdom to be ruled by a single hereditary succession. The period began with a burst of reform measures, including an attack on Buddhist institutions, a reshuffling of landownership, purges of officials of the old regime, and substitution of a new generation of educated officials chosen for their merit through the examination system. This change was at the center of a long-term shift in power and organization from the local lords and landowners of the late Silla and Koryŏ periods to a true central government supported and staffed by members of a Confucian-oriented bureaucratic class.[7]

The emphasis on promoting Confucian-educated officials was a conscious attempt to fight corruption, but it also represented a major shift in external relations with China. General Yi and his immediate descendants reorganized Korea as a loyal tributary of China, going so far as to ask the emperor to name their new state (he chose "Chosŏn") and abjectly pleading for imperial approval for the new regime, which took some time while General Yi and his sons dangled in a kind of limbo, appearing to be nothing better than usurpers. Approval came in time, when the third king of Chosŏn was "invested" by the Ming emperor, but it cannot have been pleasant to announce that Korea was henceforth going to be a loyal tributary only to be stonewalled and left to struggle and beg.

Meanwhile, to underscore the break with the past and the creation of a new regime in Korea, General Yi's court moved the government to a new location on the banks of the Han River, founding a city in 1396 that is now Seoul, the capital of South Korea. He designed his city following Chinese urban design principles and constructed a royal palace that stands today as a jewel-box version of Beijing's Forbidden City, backed by imposing mountains and standing at the head of the city's main avenue.

The attack on Buddhism within Korea meant banishing monks and temples. This was part of the explicit adoption of neo-Confucianism as the Chosŏn state's official ideology. For centuries, Confucianists in China and Korea had looked down on Buddhism as a tool for distracting the masses from the work at hand. People were supposed to think about their duties and obligations and live accordingly, not to dream about heaven and spirits or to waste money on offerings to idols. Confucianists detested the way Buddhist monks withdrew to monasteries and refused to marry or have children, thus grossly disrespecting their obligations to ancestors and their family lineages. The Confucianists thought it silly to have wasted so much effort carving the eighty-one thousand printing blocks for the *Tripitaka* not once but twice. They confiscated the wealth that many temples had collected. Even though many of the new leaders were Buddhists in their personal lives, they recognized that organized Buddhist religion had become a threat to the state and had to be suppressed. Temples were outlawed in the capital. Monks and temple slaves were "returned to their former occupations" (i.e., farming and taxpaying), and the surviving Buddhist temples were relocated in the mountains.

Moral cultivation is the heart of Confucian ideology, and in Chosŏn it was expressed through an "encouragement of learning." Neo-Confucianism stresses an understanding of reality through disciplined mental effort to achieve the "rectification of names": seeking truth from facts, acting with integrity, and saying what one means. Harmony and balance are major goals, and things that are out of balance, or acting against nature, are to be corrected. Thus, regulation and restraint are correctives for social ills. Leadership should be by example and not by force. Injustice is to be remedied through the restrained application of law and leadership.

Living in a Confucian state meant following Confucian regulations about strict segregation of the sexes. Women were legally subjected to male authority and lost the ability to act in their own behalf in matters of marriage and property. Since sons were required to carry on the family lineage, the birth of a daughter was often taken as a calamity. Few families invested in education for daughters. Very few women ever learned to read, much less acquire the ability to support themselves. They were virtual property of their fathers when they were young, of their husbands as adults, and of their sons when they grew old. And if their husbands died, even if they were only betrothed and not yet actually married, propriety required that they live as widows. It was said that a woman could not give herself to two husbands any more than an official could serve two kings.[8]

The imperatives of family lineage also led to widespread concubinage. A man whose wife failed to bear sons might take a secondary wife, or concubine. In Korean practice, however, any son borne by a concubine was subject to the stigma of illegitimacy and faced discrimination, for example, in eligibility to take the state examinations, even if he was educated and capable. Discrimination against the sons of concubines was a by-product of the patriarchy that dominated social life and mores during the Chosŏn dynasty.

A great exemplar of Confucian leadership was King Sejong, the most famous of Chosŏn's monarchs, who ruled from 1418 to 1450. He was a true scholar-king, a sponsor of important new studies in history, literature, astronomy, and philosophy. King Sejong's most important contribution was the invention of an alphabet for the Korean language, a system of writing that provided a phonetic symbol for every sound in the Korean language. The alphabet, known today as *han'gŭl* (Korean writing) has fourteen consonants and ten vowels arranged in clusters and pronounced as word syllables. The idea of writing syllables came from Chinese, but where Chinese syllable words are expressed in symbols that are sometimes actually pictures of things, Korean syllables are simply maps of sounds, as in any other phonetic alphabet.

The *han'gŭl* alphabet, of course, was not invented by King Sejong himself but by an academy of scholars known as the "Hall of Worthies," or Chiphyŏnjŏn. Sejong was unusual in his ability to hold his own with the most erudite of his advisers. He enjoyed the company of wise men and being part of their scholarly projects. One of his scholars, Chŏng Inji, wrote an official history of Koryŏ. Others invented instruments to measure weather and time. King Sejong himself sponsored major projects in fields ranging from music to mathematics. He also tried out a system of movable copper type for printing.[9]

The Chosŏn aristocracy is known by the term *yangban,* which means "two branches," referring to the civil and military branches of the bureaucracy. An office-holding *yangban* typically had passed one of the advanced examinations for his branch. Although there were still some officials who gained office by reward because they had served the king in some special way, by the early Chosŏn period most officials were suc-

Figure 2.4: Statue of King Sejong the Great, Tŏksu Palace, Seoul. Photo by Donald Clark.

cessful passers of the state examinations. And yet Korea's noble families enjoyed advantages even in the examination system. There were no public schools, and education was very expensive. Thus, the cycle tended to repeat, from education to office to wealth to more education, more office, and more wealth. The preferred form of wealth was land, so the most powerful families tended to accumulate land, not unlike the *nongjang* estates of the Koryŏ period, living on income generated by the labor of tenants and slaves.

The patterns of success in careers and wealth during the Chosŏn period generated considerable conflict within the *yangban* class. Cliques formed during crises, and alliances turned into political factions that conspired to keep competitors out of office. As the stakes rose the conflicts became violent, leading at points to bloody purges. Confucian principles were often cited as reasons to exclude evil competitors or even to have them killed. There was considerable turmoil in the course of Chosŏn's politics.[10]

The remarkable power of the *yangban* as a group reflects the corresponding weakness of Chosŏn kings. Kings started out seeking support, first from the emperor of China, who had to approve the accession of all new kings in Korea, and then from factions of the *yangban* that were needed to carry out his will in government. The *yangban* cliques perpetuated themselves through academies called *sŏwŏn*, where young scholars were trained to support their elders' ideas and political positions. In good Confucian fashion, a *sŏwŏn* graduate was expected to be a loyal follower of his mentor, who most likely had spent some time at the group's *sŏwŏn* teaching and telling stories about what had happened in Seoul. The mentor was regarded as a kind of godfather, and he protected his followers and maneuvered them into government jobs. Strong mentors with active *sŏwŏn* academies thus spread the contagion of factional fighting in the government.

The Chosŏn kingdom experienced its worst crisis, however, in the form of yet another foreign invasion. In 1592, after subjugating the feudal lords of Japan, the warlord Hideyoshi set out to create a great empire that included Korea and China. To reach China and conquer the Ming, the ruling dynasty at the time, Hideyoshi's armies had to land at Pusan in southeastern Korea and advance through Korea to the Chinese border. Korea was unprepared for the invasion and had to ask for assistance from the Ming court in Beijing. Chinese armies intervened in Korea and stopped the Japanese advance, turning the peninsula into a battlefield. The Koreans themselves resisted, first with their own army, then with local militia units organized by local *yangban* and sometimes even with Buddhist monks, although they were most often defeated by the better-trained Japanese.

Along the southern coast, however, a Korean official named Yi Sunsin carried on a most effective naval campaign, which sank many Japanese ships and disrupted the Japanese supply lines. Admiral Yi put copper canopies over the decks of his wooden boats to protect them from Japanese arrows and the burning projectiles that the Japanese used to set enemy boats on fire. Then, using oarsmen below decks, he maneuvered his boats close to the Japanese vessels and attacked them with great effectiveness. The copper canopies resembled the shells of turtles, so Admiral Yi's boats were called "turtle ships" (*kŏbuksŏn* in Korean). Admiral Yi is remembered not only for his invention but also for his daring. He used his knowledge of the coastline to trick the Japanese into entering traps where they were more easily destroyed. At the end of the war, in 1598, Admiral Yi was killed in the middle of his greatest battle. He died a hero to the Koreans, and he is remembered as their finest example of military prowess and honest sacrifice. Today his tomb is a national shrine, and his statue stands overlooking the main crossroads of downtown Seoul.

THE LATER CHOSON PERIOD, 1600–1910

The war with Japan lasted from 1592 to 1598 and ended only after Hideyoshi died and his successors abandoned his plan to rule the mainland. Korea suffered greatly from the war. Many Koreans died in the fighting, and others were captured or kidnapped and taken to Japan. There was much vandalism and looting. Many of Korea's remaining Buddhist temples were ransacked and burned. Their precious gold-leaf images and paintings were stolen not only by the Japanese enemy but also by the "friendly" Chinese. In Seoul itself, when the king and royal court fled the city just before it fell to the invading Japanese, Korean citizens, reacting to being abandoned by their ruler, attacked the central palace and set it ablaze. It is said that the fires that burned the palace's collection of documents were set by Korean slaves who wanted to destroy the records that marked them as members of the country's lowest class.

Figure 2.5: Statue of Admiral Yi Sunsin, Kwanghwamun, Seoul. Photo by Donald Clark.

The war in Korea coincided with the rise of a powerful new Manchurian state under a gifted leader named Nurhachi. Nurhachi and his sons unified the nomadic tribes formerly known as the Jurchens, organized them into fighting units, and made plans to conquer the fast-fading Ming dynasty in China. Before they did that, the Manchus, as they were called, subjugated the Koreans by invading the peninsula, first in 1627 and again in 1636, and forcing the king to swear loyalty to them. Then, with Korea under control, they found an opportunity to invade China in 1644 and overthrow the Ming government.

Having to bow to the barbarian Manchus was a bitter defeat for the Koreans, but they had little choice. Together with the Japanese invasions of the 1590s, the Manchu invasions were a serious disruption of Korean society and a blow to the state of Chosŏn. Despite this, however, the Korean system proved resilient. Although the *yangban* as a class continued to dominate society, there were important innovations in the eighteenth century. The long and peaceful reigns of Kings Yŏngjo (reigned 1724–76) and Chŏngjo (reigned 1776–1800) were a time of artistic and literary creativity. Chinese-style landscape and portrait paintings prized by the *yangban* were supplemented by new, commoner-style "genre paintings" showing ordinary people engaged in daily life. These "genre paintings" today are some of the most descriptive documents about Korea in the 1700s.

The era also brought advances in literature written in *han'gŭl* script. This followed many years during which King Sejong's alphabet was little used. Korean writers, most of them *yangban*, had scorned the alphabet as too easy and limiting, and they continued to write in the much more difficult Chinese characters that were so hard for ordinary people to learn. It took many years and a great deal of money to learn to write Chinese well. Few people who were not *yangban*-class men could afford this kind of education. Accordingly, the few who could write Chinese were able to use literacy and their writing ability as a social barrier, protecting their privileged position while denying basic communications skills to the less fortunate.

In the eighteenth century, however, the educated women who belonged to the royal family, along with other cultured women of the *yangban* class, began to write their own literature, not in Chinese but in the Korean *han'gŭl* alphabet. Their works were diaries, memoirs, and stories about palace life, written in the Korean language and far more expressive of the emotions and conflicts that were so authentically a part of daily life.[11] Certain commoners also learned *han'gŭl* well enough to write stories and novels. These works survive as commentaries on the conditions and injustices of life in the *yangban*-dominated Chosŏn kingdom, and by the nineteenth century, *han'gŭl* had become a tool for non-*yangban* to communicate and even organize rebellions against their rulers.

CHANGE WITHIN TRADITION

There has been much controversy over how to understand the later phases of the Chosŏn dynasty. One view is that by the nineteenth century it had become locked into patterns of corruption that sapped its ability to reform or adapt to the modern world. Another view is that Korea was organized to be a self-sustaining society that demonstrated considerable innovation on its own terms but was not well prepared to deal with the crisis of "internationalization" in the late 1800s that led eventually to its conquest by imperial Japan. Perhaps both views are true. In the 1920s, some Korean scholars tried to prove the latter view by reaching back into Korea's ancient history for the origins of their national values and identity. The basic purpose of their construction, or reconstruction, of Korean

Figure 2.6: Officials from the South Korean Ministry of Education reenact Confucian ceremonies in Seoul, 1983. Photo by Donald Clark.

history seems to have been to defend Korea's "nationhood," even though the modern idea of a "nation," or "nation-state" may not be the best way to describe the Koreans in ancient times or how they thought of themselves.[12]

Whatever the interpretation of Korea's past, it seems clear that the Koreans as a people, organized in families and villages and later in counties and provinces under the Chosŏn dynasty, had a well-established, self-sufficient agricultural economy organized within a bureaucratic state. Their society was very conservative and resistant to the kind of revolutionary thinking that came with the dawn of modernization, but it was resilient enough to deal with significant change.[13]

A good example of this "change within tradition" was the development, in the late 1700s, of the Silhak (Practical Learning) school of Confucian thought. Silhak was not a "modern" school of thought. It was based on the ideas of the Chinese founder of neo-Confucianism, Chu Hsi (1130–1200), who had taught that truth can be found through a better understanding of

29

reality—"the investigation of things," as he called it. In the late 1700s, a group of Korean yangban who were concerned about the breakdown of their country's land and tax systems, among other problems, embarked on a new avenue of analytical inquiry. "Practical Learning" (Silhak) was their theme, and it was influenced by information brought back from China by traveling tribute envoys regarding Western scientific ideas. The traveling Koreans learned that Chinese intellectuals had been enjoying a lively conversation with westerners—Jesuit missionaries—regarding scientific fields such as physics and mathematics. The Koreans likewise were intrigued by Western approaches to studies of the natural world and, inevitably, the philosophical questions that came with them, including even the religious messages of Christianity. Above all, the Silhak scholars wanted realistic answers to the problems facing Korea, even if it meant adopting Western science and technology. They also went far toward adopting the Jesuits' understanding of the spiritual dimension and even founded their own branch of the Catholic religion in Seoul, which turned out to be the beginning of Korean Christianity.

Silhak thought stands as an example of what might have been, but in the Korea of that time it was entangled with factional politics and an official horror of heterodoxy within the power structure (i.e., Korean conservatism). The fact that some of the Silhak thinkers took up Christianity and (more important) wanted to modify Confucian practice essentially reduced them to criminals in the Korean system. For example, when the first Korean Catholics stopped "worshipping" their ancestors in the sacred Confucian family ritual known as the *chesa*, they were labeled as immoral and even punished with death. Indeed, there was a backlash movement in Korea, called the "resist heresy, support orthodoxy" (*chŏksa wijŏng*) movement, which encouraged people to report on deviants such as Christians and help bring them to justice. There were bloody purges throughout much of the century, bringing death to hundreds, and in 1866 thousands, of "heretics."[14]

THE "OPENING" AND COLONIZATION OF KOREA

Korea remained isolated from the outside world throughout most of the nineteenth century, content to maintain its special relationship with China and to be left alone. There were outbreaks of dissatisfaction in the form of peasant revolts, and an uprising of unhappy miners in northwestern Korea nearly became a civil war.[15] In the 1860s a religious leader in the southwest founded the "Religion of the Heavenly Way" (Ch'ŏndogyo), recruited thousands of peasants, and briefly threatened central control over

Figure 2.7: Hyangwŏnjŏng Pavilion and Lotus Pond, Kyŏngbok Palace, Seoul
Photo by Donald Clark.

his region. There were attempts by British, French, and American naval vessels to pierce Korea's shell and open a dialogue, but these ended in failure. In 1876 the Japanese sent a warship, which forced the Koreans to sign a treaty opening trade and diplomatic relations with Japan. Additional treaties followed in the 1880s with the United States, Great Britain, Germany, Russia, and France, among others. Included in the treaties were provisions lifting the ban on Christianity, and before long Western missionaries, Protestants and Catholics, took up residence in Korea's main cities and towns, founding churches, starting schools, and building clinics and hospitals. In addition, a handful of adventurous Western investors put their money into Korean gold mines and railroad concessions, helping lay the foundation of Korean economic modernization.

By the early twentieth century, several Western countries had established a small stake in Korea. Their interests were small compared to those of Japan, however, which looked on Korea as a strategic territory that could not be allowed to fall into the hands of a potential enemy. In 1895 Japan won the Sino-Japanese War and forced the Chinese to renounce their historic tributary relationship with Korea. In 1905 Japan won the

Figure 2.8: Kojong and Sunjong, the last two monarchs of the Chosŏn dynasty. Photograph courtesy of the Willard Dickerman Straight and Early U.S.-Korea Diplomatic Relations collection, Cornell University Library.

Russo-Japanese War and forced the Russians to declare an end to their interests in Korea. These Japanese victories, together with Korea's own military weakness and the lack of any outside power willing to step in and defend the country, set the stage for Japan to assert a "protectorate" over Korea. In 1910 Japan completed the process of conquest and forced the Koreans to sign another treaty ceding their country to Japan as an outright possession. From that point until the end of World War Two, Korea was a colony of Japan.[16]

3

KOREA'S COLONIAL ORDEAL,
1910–1945

Ships, guns, and ambition for world power were the main drivers of Japan's success in overwhelming the kingdom of Chosŏn at the beginning of the twentieth century. Japan was able to move on Korea because of international conditions: elimination of China as Korea's defender in 1895; elimination of Russia as a rival for power in the region in 1905; and the indifference or inability of other powers, including Great Britain and the United States. The United States, for example, signed an agreement in 1905 promising not to interfere with Japan's ambitions in Korea if Japan would not interfere with American colonial rule in the Philippines.

At the time, Japanese planners thought of Korea as a "dagger pointed at the heart of Japan" and that no other power should be allowed to wield the dagger. Beyond that, they engaged in a long-running argument over the value of Korea to Japan and the potential costs and benefits of ruling it directly. In the 1890s, Japan thought it had an overpopulation problem and tried to boost emigration to Hawaii and North America. Korea, however, was too poor and populated to attract many Japanese immigrants. Beyond Korea, however, lay Manchuria, the underpopulated homeland of the Manchus, who were ruling China. Manchuria was rich in land, minerals, forests, water power, and all the essential elements of agriculture and industry. So whether Japan's leaders saw Korea as valuable in itself or as a stepping stone to the eventual conquest of Manchuria, the victories over China (1895) and Russia (1905) created an opportunity that Japan simply could not afford to miss.

In 1905, Japan declared Korea a "protectorate" and bullied the Korean government into signing over Chosŏn's foreign relations and defenses. It is significant, as a sign of how seriously the Japanese regarded their Korean project in 1905, that they assigned their greatest statesman, Itō Hirobumi, the author of Japan's modern constitution and its first prime minister, to supervise the Korean protectorate as its "resident-general." Itō disarmed the royal Korean army, opened the door to Japanese investment and land development, and promoted transportation and communications in a way designed to enable the Japanese to extract Korea's crops and minerals. In 1907, after a brief protest by the Korean king, Itō took over Korea's internal administration, finances, and courts, extending Japan's control over Korea's main levers of government. A Korean assassin killed Itō in 1909, an event that spurred Japan to complete the process of colonization. On August 22, 1910, Japanese officers persuaded Korea's top ministers to sign a Treaty of Annexation, which made Korea part of Japan.

During their first decade of colonial rule in Korea, the Japanese changed many things. They abolished the monarchy, bribed many of the wealthy *yangban* in order to win their support, rounded up and shot many former Korean soldiers who had become part of a resistance movement, and tried to intimidate everyone who did not accept or support their dominance. The Korean colony's first two rulers—who held the title of governor-general—were both hard-line army generals. Functioning as dictators, with executive, legislative, and judicial power concentrated in their hands, they ruled with very little supervision from Tokyo. They issued numerous orders regulating the press, education, assembly, and a number of basic rights nominally guaranteed to Japanese citizens under the Meiji Constitution of 1889. There was a new land survey, which resulted in many Korean farmers losing their property to a Japanese development company, which usually sold it to Japanese who came over in search of cheap land.[1] To enforce their edicts they used a military police force known as the Kempeitai and a system of courts under martial law that took little notice of human rights. Korea was reorganized to serve Japan, and the Koreans themselves were reduced to low-paid workers in their own country.

On March 1, 1919, a coalition of Korean religious leaders organized a peaceful protest against the harsh policies of the Japanese colonial government and demanded independence for Korea. The Japanese colonial authorities met the protests with force, and for nearly a year there were clashes, often violent, between the people and Japanese troops. Ultimately the March First Independence Movement, as it is known, cost the lives of more than seven thousand Koreans. The movement did not win independence for Korea, but it did lead to a softening of Japanese colonial policies. Japanese politicians were embarrassed before the world when Koreans proved willing to fight and die to end the "benefits" of Japanese rule. The harsh decade of martial law therefore came to an end.

34

The governor-general during the 1920s was Saitō Makoto, a retired navy admiral whose style was more humane. Saitō allowed Koreans to hold meetings and publish their own magazines and newspapers. He improved education and allowed Koreans to have a government-sponsored university. He let them join religious and even political organizations. Koreans used this period to discuss how they should continue pushing for independence. Some said that the Japanese were too strong to be defeated and would have to be accepted while Koreans tried to preserve their culture through studies of history and literature and by educating young Koreans to work toward liberation. These are sometimes referred to as the "cultural nationalists." Others argued that the only way to get rid of the Japanese was to take up weapons and fight. They worked to organize associations, whether legal or illegal, that empowered farmers, workers, and the small bands of guerrillas that did the fighting. Both the cultural nationalists and the advocates of armed struggle had support from abroad. The cultural nationalists were supported by overseas Koreans in China and the United States. The armed revolutionaries were supported by people in the Soviet Union and communists in Manchuria and China.[2]

During the early 1930s Japan launched its armed expansion beyond Korea. Korea became a staging area for the invasion of Manchuria in 1931–32 and China itself in 1937. Only a few Koreans served in the Japanese

朝鮮總督府 (所名城京)
The Government General of Chosen, Keijo.

Figure 3.1: The Government-General of Chōsen Building, the Japanese colonial headquarters in Seoul. Collection of the author.

forces at first. In the 1930s they were mainly drafted as laborers in Japan's factories and mines to replace workers who were drafted into the military services to do the actual fighting. More than a million Koreans were taken to Japan to work, and many of their descendants continue to live there, as we have seen. The labor draft for Koreans involved women as well as men. Some were sent abroad along with Japan's army to serve the troops in the field as cooks and laundresses. Many others were recruited and even kidnapped and forced to serve as sex slaves for the soldiers in the war zone. The Japanese called them "comfort women."[3]

Part of the mobilization that the Japanese forced on the Koreans was meant to make them better subjects of Japanese emperor Hirohito. They were ordered to go to shrines and pay their respects to the spirits of the war dead and Japan's national heroes. They were ordered to speak Japanese and stop speaking Korean. They were ordered to change their names and begin identifying themselves as Japanese. Some of the cultural nationalists who had been trying to keep Korean culture alive were arrested and forced to speak out in support of Japan's imperial plan. And during the war itself Koreans were forced to make great material sacrifices, enduring food rationing and contributing pots and pans and even their jewelry as the war gobbled up every bit of metal that could be located in the Japanese empire. When clothing wore out it simply was patched and patched again until the Koreans were wearing rags. When shoes wore out people made straw shoes or went barefoot.

Colonialism as a worldwide phenomenon corrupted many societies, and Korea under Japan was no exception. Force and intimidation were essential elements, forms of state terrorism by Japanese occupiers over the Korean people, who lived in constant fear of the Kempeitai and the colonial police. Second was the economic misdevelopment of the colony in ways designed to help extract Korea's crops, minerals, and other resources for use by Japan. Japan introduced modern education, communications, transportation, electric power, industry, banking, and retail marketing to Korea but mainly reserved the benefits for the Japanese in Korea and Japan itself. Few Koreans were allowed to rise very high in these modern systems or to manage their operations. Japan thus disrupted Korean life with modern things while holding Koreans in place as second-class citizens in their own country. The legal guarantees of human rights in the Japanese Constitution were never extended to Koreans in the colony. Japanese-run schools limited the number of Koreans admitted; indeed, only one in five Korean children had ever seen the inside of a school when the occupation finally ended in 1945. Koreans were exhorted to be "good Japanese," to worship Japan's deities at Shintō shrines, and even to take new Japanese names for themselves, but they never could escape their subjection under Japanese military and police control. Even in the military, it was only after Japan was desperate for manpower that Koreans were recruited in significant numbers, and then they were mainly assigned to the imperial army in Manchuria, away from Japan, or to occupied lands in the Pacific, where they were employed in menial jobs, for example, as prison guards.

One type of damage to Korea was psychological: the planting of the idea that Japanese were better than Koreans. Many Koreans became used to admiring Japanese and trying to imitate them, coveting their discipline, sense of purpose, and modern skills. Even after the war, when Korea was independent, there was a tendency to look up to Japan even while denouncing the colonial regime. There is much Japanese influence in the way Koreans did things after 1945, whether in schools, the military, business and banking, transportation, or even popular culture. In South Korea it took many decades for people to devise their own style of being Korean. In the north as well, the miseries of life under Japanese oppression continue to influence the way history is taught and public policy is formulated.

The most corrosive and corrupting aspect of Japanese rule was and remains the legacy of collaboration. The fact is that many Koreans, south and north, resigned themselves to "being Japanese" in the 1930s and 1940s. Not seeing much hope for Korean independence, they settled down and began obeying colonial laws and doing as they were told by the colonial authorities. In some cases they were rewarded or met success doing business the Japanese way, and when Korea suddenly was liberated in 1945, these people—now accused of collaboration—suffered much public outrage for having prospered under colonial rule. The stain of collaboration colored landlords, businessmen, Koreans in the colonial police and army, educators, journalists, artists and writers, and many members of the former *yangban* nobility.

In the Soviet-occupied northern zone, discrimination against people accused of collaboration was so severe that many were forced to flee to the south. Landowners who had managed to hold on to their property through the colonial period were stripped of their holdings during a sweeping land reform program. They were among entire categories of people who found themselves blacklisted by the new regime. Others included "capitalists" who owned businesses and were accused of exploiting workers and Christians who at first opposed the officially atheist socialist regime and had a political party of their own that briefly tried to rival the socialists. Many people in these endangered categories decided to take what they could carry and move to the southern zone, where they had to start from scratch and remained for generations as vocal members of a virulently anticommunist South Korean system.

South Korea, too, had its share of former collaborators. However, under the American military government, private property, anticommunism, and business success were not crimes, and in fact the Americans depended on people who had risen under the Japanese to carry forward the kinds of law, order, and economic activity that the United States wanted to see in the southern occupation zone. For example, when it came to laying the groundwork for what later became the Republic of Korea Army (ROKA), the Americans turned to Korean officers who had served in the Japanese imperial forces, taught them English, and put them in charge of the early Korean "constabulary." One of the constabulary's first missions was to seek out and destroy pockets of leftist activity in the southern zone: peasant and labor unions, strikers, and communist "cells."

In the years just after liberation, therefore, a curious dynamic emerged in the South Korean system, consisting of elites who had collaborated with the Japanese struggling to prove their patriotism after the fact. The first South Korean republic under President Syngman Rhee, for example, was populated with Korean officials who would have been blacklisted as "collaborators" in the north but were put in charge of government ministries because they had business and administrative experience. The Rhee regime therefore had to try to overcome the taint of collaboration by following strongly anti-Japanese policies that were sometimes wasteful or even silly. For example, Rhee asserted that Korean territorial waters extended fully halfway across the East Sea and threatened to seize any Japanese fishing boats that tried to come across the "Rhee Line." He demanded apologies, reparations, and the repatriation of Koreans living in Japan; he refused any kind of military cooperation with Japan even to defend against Communist China and North Korea; and at one point he even ordered Korea's clocks moved back half an hour so that Korea would not have to share a time zone with Japan.

In these ways, the South Korean state that was founded in 1948 took shape as the creation of an American-backed conservative class of Koreans, some of whom were vulnerable to attack for their earlier coexistence, or collaboration, with the Japanese colonial regime. The North Korean regime has always made much of this fact to attack the legitimacy of South Korea, and in the south itself there is still plenty of controversy on this point. Indeed, the keeping of lists of alleged collaborators and their descendants is a kind of industry in South Korea, with books published every year naming names and describing what the collaborators did, even if they were never actually found guilty or punished. In the 1990s, for example, a leading presidential candidate in two elections was forced to defend his father's service as a Korean judge in a colonial court, and it is widely believed that this fact cost the candidate success in both elections. The fallout from this problem remains an important factor in Korean political affairs well into the twenty-first century.

4

KOREA AS A DIVIDED NATION

In August 1945, the Allied powers won the Pacific War and stripped Japan of its empire. Korea was liberated, like Taiwan and other holdings from long before the war, and Koreans throughout their land rejoiced at the news that they were going to be free. However, they soon learned that their liberation really only meant a new kind of foreign occupation. The United States and the Soviet Union, believing that the Korean people were not ready to govern themselves, had agreed to divide the peninsula along a line across the middle—along the thirty-eighth parallel of north latitude—creating two occupation zones, the north for the Soviet Union and the south for the United States. Koreans thus watched in dismay as new foreign armies took control of their land.

Looking back, it seems presumptuous for the Americans and Soviets to have thought that Korea was unfit to govern itself—since it had done so for centuries before 1910. The facts show that Allied planners knew next to nothing about Korea in August of 1945. Nor did they consult any Koreans as they looked at the map and picked the line that would divide the peninsula in two. Instead they simply looked on Korea as a former Japanese asset that warranted military occupation pending a decision about how to dispose of it, and they casually created a major human tragedy.

HOW KOREA WAS DIVIDED

It is important to remember that in mid-1945 the United States and the Soviet Union were still allies and that the United States had strongly urged the Soviet Union to declare war on Japan in order to help end the Pacific War. The events of August 1945 followed in quick succession: the nuclear bombing of Hiroshima on August 6, the Soviet declaration of war against Japan on August 8, the nuclear bombing of Nagasaki on August 9, Japan's decision to surrender on August 12, and the surrender announcement on August 15. The Soviet Union quickly took the southern half of Sakhalin and the Kurile Islands, engaged Japanese forces in Manchuria, and sent troops into northern Korea, alarming American planners about the possibility that Soviet forces might become involved in the occupation of Japan itself.

Embracing the concept of a shared occupation of the region, including Manchuria, the Korean Peninsula, and Japan proper, the United States proposed the following: the United States to occupy Japan, the Soviet Union to occupy Manchuria, and the two Allied armies to share in the occupation of Korea by dividing the peninsula into two zones at the thirty-eighth parallel. The Soviet Union would thereby recover what it had lost in the Russo-Japanese War of 1904–5, the United States would get its wish to be the sole occupier of the Japanese home islands, and the Koreans would get a "trusteeship" in which the two trustees would consult to work out a plan for a reunited and independent Korean nation.

Thus it happened that the Soviet Red Army occupied northern Korea down to the thirty-eighth parallel in August 1945, and the following month American troops arrived to occupy the south. The victorious allies accepted the surrender of Japanese forces and set about exercising their trusteeships in their respective zones. Each side sought out like-minded Koreans and used them to help govern. The unfortunate result, virtually from the beginning, was the fostering of incompatible Korean regimes in the two zones, the one in the north modeled on Russian socialism and the one in the south modeled on American democratic capitalism. That is how Korea came to be divided, and no one yet has figured out a way to put it back together.

In the first days after the end of the war, Japanese personnel in Korea ran for cover. So did the Korean police who had worked for them. In the weeks before the occupying Allied armies were able to take control, Korean communities in both zones organized informal "peacekeeping" groups on their own, basically to keep order but also to catch and punish criminals, including collaborators. The most common of these were "people's committees" (*inmin wiwŏnhoe*), which went beyond peacekeeping and began planning programs for land redistribution and other political and social changes that could easily have been labeled "communist." When the Allied armies arrived to take over in their respective zones, they supplanted the people's committees and established their own authority. However, in the north, because the objectives of the people's committees were often far to the left, the Soviet authorities retained them as elements of the system. This was in contrast to the south, where the people's committees were confronting the elites as enemies of the people and seeking to redistribute their wealth. These elites quickly formed themselves into a political coalition that sought out the American authorities to convince them that the rabble in the people's committees was essentially communist. This triggered an American military response that developed into an outright repression campaign against the South Korean Left—the people's committees and unions of farmers and industrial workers—that mainly eliminated it as a factor in the southern political system. In other words, the South Korean right wing—the leading conservatives—succeeded in co-opting the American military government in maintaining the existing arrangements of wealth and power.[1]

In the early months of the southern occupation, the conservative coalition of business leaders and landowners, former independence movement figures, and ethnic Koreans returning from China and the United States, including American-educated Christians, persuaded U.S. authorities to drop their support of the trusteeship plan in favor of outright independence at the earliest possible date. When the Americans changed their view on trusteeship, the Soviet side accused the United States of breaking the bargain and trying to split southern Korea off from the north. From that point until the present, the North Korean side has always argued that the existence of the South Korean republic is illegitimate, the product of a broken bargain and the creature of a privileged faction of Koreans who oppose social justice and meaningful reform in the way wealth and power are distributed in Korean society.

With the collapse of the trusteeship formula for Korean reunification and with the failure of the two occupying authorities to devise an alternate plan for Korean self-government, the Soviets proceeded with the installation of communist-leaning Koreans in the north while the Americans promoted anticommunist Koreans in the south. Syngman Rhee, an American-educated independence figure who had spent many years in exile in the United States, emerged as the front-runner in the south. Kim Il-sung, a Pyongyang native who had served in the Soviet Red Army as a major in an ethnic Korean unit, was hand-picked to become the leader in the north. Although each leader—Rhee and Kim—had credentials in the struggle for independence from Japan, they represented opposite poles of Korean politics and neither was acceptable to the opposite side. With the emergence of the cold war between 1945 and 1948, Rhee and Kim came to represent the reality that had developed in Korea, a postcolonial local struggle between the Korean Left and Right that metastasized into the creation of rival countries poised to serve as surrogates in the global conflict between East and West.

ORIGINS OF THE KOREAN WAR

Thus were born the two republics: the Republic of Korea (ROK) in the south and the Democratic People's Republic of Korea (DPRK) in the north. It did not take long to set the stage for war between them. In 1947, following an American decision to end its occupation of the south, the United States turned to the United Nations to organize a national plebiscite in Korea to determine which of the two governments would remain as the permanent political authority. For the United States, this was a way to cover withdrawal from an unwanted commitment and test the power of the newly created United Nations to solve difficult international problems. For the North Korean side, however, the proposal seemed to be a clever attempt to impose an American-determined outcome on the Korean situation. For one thing, there were twice as many voters in South Korea under the presumed control of American authorities. As it turned out, therefore, the UN-sponsored election took place only in the southern zone, in May of 1948. This created a constitutional assembly, which elected Syngman Rhee, universally regarded as the American candidate, as president of the Republic of Korea. In the following month, September 1948, Kim Il-sung proclaimed the establishment of the Democratic People's Republic of Korea in the north. Soviet and American forces pulled out of Korea but continued to support their Korean clients as the thirty-eighth parallel hardened into a dangerous military frontier.

As the American occupation forces pulled out, they donated their weapons and equipment to the brand-new South Korean army, hoping that the South Koreans could sustain themselves in the event of open hostilities. Kim Il-sung, meanwhile, believed that South Koreans, if given a free choice, would prefer to live under the northern regime, which he asserted had more legitimate roots in the long struggle against Japan. South Korean communists assured him that the right combination of aid and military pressure from the north would touch off a spontaneous rebellion in the south against the conservative regime of Syngman Rhee. Despite attempts to make this happen, it never did. By 1950, Kim seemed to have only one option left: a direct invasion to "liberate" South Korea.

After getting assurances of Soviet and Chinese Communist support, Kim ordered the Korean People's Army into action across the line on June 25, 1950. This invasion began the Korean War, a three-year episode that killed or wounded more than 3 million people, including more than 2 million Koreans, 900,000 Chinese, 57,000 Americans (including 34,000 combat deaths), and several thousand from the various countries that joined under the United Nations' flag to punish the North Koreans for attacking their "neighbor."[2]

The United Nations' role in the Korean War was the first major UN intervention in a world crisis, aimed at proving the capability of the organization to deal with disruptions of the peace by international aggressors. With the Soviet representative absent and therefore unable to cast a veto, the remaining members of the UN Security Council passed two resolutions, one demanding that the North Koreans stop their invasion and, when that went unheeded, a second one creating an international army led by the United States to enter the conflict and repel the invaders. The United States and fifteen other UN member states sent soldiers to participate. Of these the largest forces by far were South Korean and American.

Figure 4.1: *Brothers*, the statue at the Korean War Memorial, Seoul. Photo by Donald Clark.

Kim's invasion seemed easy for a few weeks, although it failed to capture all of South Korea. The Americans, meanwhile, organized a counterattack that succeeded in wiping out most of the North Korean army and occupying much of North Korea by November. It was at this point that the Chinese entered the war, not wanting to see the destruction of a neighboring communist country, feeling that they owed a debt to the Korean Communists who had helped them win their own civil war against the Chinese Nationalists in the 1940s, and fearing that the Americans would invade China next. The Chinese intervention changed the direction of the war again, forcing the Americans, South Koreans, and United Nations halfway down the Korean Peninsula, more or less to the thirty-eighth parallel, where the war settled down to a two-year stalemate. It ended with a truce on July 27, 1953.

THE MEANING OF THE KOREAN WAR

During most of the cold war, especially in South Korea and the United States, the story of the Korean War, including the period prior to the North Korean invasion when the South Korean state was being created under American direction, was highly distorted and politicized. During that time, the United States and South Korea placed all the blame for the catastrophe on North Korea and represented the conflict as an act of international aggression that the law-abiding international community had to answer with military force. Lessons learned in World War Two—the lesson of Munich, for example, when a German aggressor was "appeased," only to grow stronger for a war that was much more destructive later on—were cited to justify the "civilized world's" response to Kim Il-sung's aggression. For decades it was difficult—even forbidden, in South Korea—to say out loud that the North Korean regime had any legitimacy when it tried to reunify the peninsula. People were required to speak of the North Korean regime as illegitimate, forced on its people against their will, puppets of bigger communist nations and deserving of defeat at the earliest moment. In the United States it was understood to have been a Soviet probe of American resolve to resist communist expansion following the "loss of China" to Communist Party rule in 1949. Americans were not encouraged to see the Korean War as an internal conflict between Koreans but rather as a battle in the global cold war.

When the truce ended the fighting in Korea, the country remained as before, divided along a line that lay fairly close to the original boundary at the thirty-eighth parallel. Under the terms of the 1953 armistice, a four-kilometer-wide strip called the Demilitarized Zone (DMZ) was created to stretch the entire width of the Korean Peninsula along the battle line as of the signing. The two warring armies were ordered to separate along this line and to refrain from any further provocative actions. Almost immediately they commenced harassments that have continued in both directions until this day. Meanwhile at a special "truce village" called Panmunjŏm, in the DMZ, the two sides traded accusations and occasionally tried to make progress toward reunification, for nearly fifty years without result. As long as the cold war continued, China and the Soviet Union backed Kim Il-sung's North Korea while the United States backed South Korea under a succession of presidents and generals.

Because of the overriding need to assure military security on both sides of the DMZ, both North and South Korea committed immense proportions of their national budgets to defense. With help from their cold

Figure 4.2 The Korean War. Map courtesy of Diane Smith.

war patrons on both sides, they modernized their armies and trained their soldiers, ostensibly for defense and deterrence, although each viewed the other as wanting to resume the Korean War as soon as it discerned that it had an advantage.

In reality, both sides were so ruined by the war that a renewed conflict was beyond the capability of either one. The Soviets and Chinese on the northern side, and the Americans on the southern side, acted to restrain the two Korean governments from engaging in any further military adventures. However, though shattered economically, in both South and North Korea defense considerations put the military first, with the armies claiming the food, clothes, ammunition, equipment, fuel, and construction materials necessary to maintain first-quality forces. Although it cost both societies dearly in terms of plans deferred and lower priorities for such things as education, public health, transportation, housing, and consumer goods, by the late 1950s armies in both parts of Korea were the most advanced and best organized elements of their respective societies.

In South Korea, considerable political conflict developed around the corruption and incompetence of the Syngman Rhee regime. Those who hoped for democratic development were disappointed as election after election proved to be occasions for the ruling group to perpetuate its grip on power. After an obviously rigged election in 1960, people began rising against the ruling group, and in April of that year public anger boiled over in a revolution that ousted Rhee and his supporters. A new constitution and government that summer seemed to promise a new era of openness and progress. However, the new government also failed to overcome the myriad economic and political problems in South Korea. It came as no surprise, therefore, that in May of 1961 units of the South Korean army, asserting concerns about economic malaise and political corruption, seized power in a coup d'état.

THE RISE OF SOUTH KOREA

The leader of the May 16, 1961, military coup in South Korea, General Park Chung-hee, vowed to lead his country out of the poverty and suffering that had plagued its people since the war. He cracked down on corruption and exhorted his people to work hard and save for the future. He created a central Economic Planning Board (EPB) and used his power to open doors to foreign money, borrowing capital and negotiating for aid from the United States and Japan. Beginning with this, the EPB mapped out a series of five-year plans that set ambitious targets for production. Using the slogan "Production, Exports, Construction!" the government made the Korean economy produce goods that could be sold abroad, earning foreign exchange that could be used to buy imported raw materials, machines, and advanced equipment for further production. The Park government also sent Korean workers to Europe and the Middle East to earn money in places where labor was scarce. In the 1960s Korean troops fought in Vietnam, their expenses paid by the United States. These multiple sources of revenue from outside Korea "primed the pump" of the Korean economy and made it possible to exceed the five-year plan targets time after time.

The government also stressed rural development through a program called the New Community Movement. Aimed at increasing agricultural productivity and raising the standard of living in the countryside, the New Community Movement made credit available to farmers; supplied them with seeds, fertilizers, and pesticides; installed electricity and safe water; promoted public health; paved roads; built schools; and improved transportation and communications. These improvements, together with the trend toward urbanization, dramatically increased per capita production in the provinces and narrowed the gap in living standards between Koreans who lived in the cities and rural villages.

Figure 4.3. Park Chung-hee, South Korean leader from 1961 to 1979, was credited with South Korea's economic growth in the 1960s and 1970s, but he was also criticized for his authoritarian rule.

The enormous sacrifices required to accomplish these things were not evenly distributed despite the government's best efforts. Many Koreans suffered under brutal working conditions. The rate of injuries and accidents among those who did "3-D" kinds of work (difficult, dirty, and dangerous), workers such as miners and those who worked in urban sweatshops, was very high. One type of worker was especially exploited: the teenage girls fresh from middle school whose good health and quick reflexes made them excellent factory hands. These girls normally worked long hours for low pay and often were expected to send their wages home to their families, sometimes to finance their brothers' educations, until they quit work to get married. Then younger girls were recruited to take their places. Korean workers were discouraged from organizing unions or engaging in any kind of collective bargaining. Indeed, their low wages were a key to South Korea's economic progress.

On the other hand, the Park government tried to engineer the success of Korea's biggest companies by having government-controlled banks make them government-guaranteed loans. These companies quickly became conglomerates, called *chaebŏl*, which were comprised of families of companies. The Hyundai *chaebŏl*, for example, includes automobile, construction, shipbuilding, and retailing components. Samsung, which started out in textiles, developed an electronics manufacturing specialty that became known around the world, first for televisions and microwave ovens and then for semiconductors and other high-tech computer components. Demand for Korean products overseas helped free Korea from foreign aid and then enriched the *chaebŏl*, enabling them to buy up smaller companies and grow big enough to control a significant part of the national economy.

When workers saw the wealth that was accumulating in the *chaebŏl*, they demanded higher wages. The Park government, however, resisted any loosening of control over the workforce. It argued that worker unrest was a threat to national security that would destabilize the country and invite intervention by Communist North Korea. Park used the national security argument to make himself a virtual dictator by 1974, ruling by decree and outlawing all criticism of himself or his style. In 1979, in the middle of a wave of worker unrest, he was assassinated by one of his own deputies. There followed a brief period of democratic reform before another army general, Chun Doo-hwan, seized power for himself. When civilians marched in the streets to protest Chun's coup, he ordered army units to attack them. After a massacre in May 1980, which killed hundreds of protesters in the city of Kwangju, the Korean people glumly allowed him to postpone democratization.

South Korea endured Chun Doo-hwan's regime from 1980 until 1987, when massive public protests turned Korea from an outright military dictatorship into something more democratic. During that period the people continued to work hard, the *chaebŏl* continued to grow, Korean products were sold all over the world, and the standard of living rose dramatically. Koreans were also proud to have Seoul chosen to host the 1988 Summer Olympic Games. Much of their energy was channeled into making the games a kind of "coming-out party" for Korea. In 1988 the world saw the games hosted in a city that had completely recovered from the war and been transformed into a thriving modern metropolis.

A year before the Olympics, however, mass demonstrations and demands from people in every walk of life forced the outgoing Chun Doo-hwan to allow a basic change in the national constitution that opened the way for unprecedented freedom. Instead of being chosen by a government-controlled electoral college, the next president would be chosen by popular vote. Among the other democratic changes, perhaps

Figure 4.4: The Hyundai shipyard in Ulsan. Photo courtesy of Franke Johnson.

the most important was the lifting of restrictions on the press. The result was a more responsive and responsible political system. And while a former army general nevertheless won the 1987 presidential election, in the 1992 and 1997 elections the winners were leaders of the opposition who were famous for having stood up to Park and Chun in the struggle for democracy during the long, dark years of military rule. The election of Kim Dae-jung as president in 1997 was especially significant. Kim Dae-jung had been a nemesis to the military leaders who preceded him. He had opposed Park Chung-hee in two elections, nearly winning one. Park had imprisoned him, and Park's police had tried to kill him more than once. Chun sentenced Kim to death in 1980, and it had taken an international outcry to get the sentence lifted.

After years as an outsider, Kim Dae-jung triumphed in the 1997 election only to be faced with the most serious economic crisis in South Korea since the Korean War. He had spoken for many years about the need for "economic democracy" in his country and had criticized the cozy symbiosis that existed between big business and previous governments. This marriage of government and big business had led to "crony capitalism" and a series of bad economic decisions, which precipitated a crash in the autumn of 1997. Just days before Kim's election, Koreans were obliged to watch in humiliation as the outgoing government sought billions of

Figure 4.5: Ch'ŏnggye-ch'ŏn Riverwalk, downtown Seoul. Photo by Donald Clark.

dollars of bailout funds from the International Monetary Fund (IMF) to cover the bad debts that had financed some of the cozy dealings of Korea's biggest companies. In return for the bailout, the IMF demanded control of certain elements of the Korean economy such as banking. When he took office in early 1998, President Kim Dae-jung was forced to begin his presidency by asking the people to accept painful levels of unemployment, the closure of badly run banks and businesses, and a sell-off of ill-conceived ventures by the big Korean conglomerates such as Hyundai and Samsung. The strong medicine took effect within a year of the crash, and by mid-1999 the Korean economy was well along the road to recovery. Although many Korean workers had not yet found jobs, the signs pointed to a better-run Korean economy in the next century, and there was plenty of reason to hope that the country would return to its former level of prosperity. President Kim Dae-jung deserved part of the credit for this, but once again it was the Korean people themselves who proved they had the discipline to meet the crisis with hard work and determination.

The story of postwar South Korea therefore is an example of state leadership combined with the power of market incentives, formidable social organization and discipline, and determined sacrifices by workers to transform the country from near starvation to one of the most productive and prosperous societies in the world.

5

NORTH KOREA

THE PEOPLE AND THEIR SYSTEM

North Korea as a news item invariably conjures up images of threat: of goose-stepping soldiers on parade in Pyongyang's Kim Il-sung Square, of rockets on display, and of scientists in white lab coats adjusting controls on atomic reactors. During his years as leader there was usually an image somewhere of the odd and inscrutable leader Kim Jong-il, suggesting that he was abnormal and therefore a danger to other inhabitants of planet Earth. These stereotypes of North Korea are deeply ingrained in minds all around the world, particularly in the United States. Similar images will continue to appear on television screens around the world as North Korea undergoes the transition to new leadership under the youthful Kim Jong-un. Like most stereotypes, they have some basis in fact, but they have not served us very well in the past and do not work very well as grounds for understanding what is really going in North Korea or for making policy about how to deal with it.

Public ignorance about North Korea and its people enables policymakers and the media to get away with sloppy analogies to make dubious points. It benefits no one to put North Korea outside the pale of "civilized nations" and call it a "headless beast" deserving to be destroyed, as *Newsweek* magazine did in 1994, upon the death of North Korea's founder Kim Il-sung.[1] The "headless beast" characterization came at a moment when the world was deeply troubled about North Korea's nuclear program and North Korea itself was in a state of shock over the founder's death. Demonizing the North Koreans made it easier to consider a preemptive attack to "decapitate" the North Korean regime, a thing that nearly happened in the Clinton administration at that time (1994) and again later during the George W. Bush administration (2003). In both cases, it was easy to see that the American leaders were not well informed about North Korea or the consequences of war, should they choose it.

In both cases the public seemed to support a "military solution" to the "problem" of North Korea. Yet if either Clinton or Bush had chosen war, it is likely that more than a million people would have died within the first twenty-four hours and millions more within the first week. Tens of thousands of Americans, including military personnel and U.S. citizens living peacefully in South Korea, would have been among the casualties.

It is often said that no military plan ever survives actual contact with the enemy.[2] Military planners in Korea certainly cannot predict what would happen after the opening salvos of a renewed Korean War, especially if the objective of "decapitating" the North Korean regime is not achieved within a few minutes or hours. Nor can anyone predict what the reaction of South Korea would be, or that of China, Japan, or Russia, all states with interests in the security of the region and the consequences of any attempt to destroy North Korea. Indeed, the only really predictable result of any such course would be unspeakable disaster on an unprecedented scale. Thus it is reckless to speak of a "military option" in Korea for it is completely impractical for all involved. Surely smart people can figure out how to make better policy than something that points to guaranteed disaster.

The Democratic People's Republic of Korea is now suffering a renewed system shock following the sudden death of the "Great General" Kim Jong-il. As a practical matter it seems likely that the world will have to live with North Korea as it is, at least for a while longer, while the country's leaders rally their people and gather whatever elements of stability they have. The year 2012 was planned to be a celebration in North Korea, marking the centennial of Kim Il-sung's birth on April 15. After long periods of struggle for survival, the DPRK was putting a high priority on construction projects and nationwide observances to mark the country's emergence as a "Great Power" under the wise leadership of Kim Jong-il. Uncertainty about the future clouds these plans; nevertheless the people of North Korea appear to remain resolute in their determination to defend their country and support their state against threats from abroad that they believe are determined to destroy them. This is a powerful incentive, but it does not begin to answer the questions that the world has about the sustainability of the North Korean system.

Whatever Kim Jong-il's faults, he was at least a leader to whom we had grown accustomed, and his regime displayed patterns that made its actions at least somewhat predictable. As he aged, the world fretted about what would happen when he passed from power. However, planners in the West missed many opportunities to open dialogue with the DPRK and move away from confrontation toward steps that might help the North Koreans embrace change and eventual reform. We know much more about North Korea than we used to, but we still isolate it and condemn it, apparently without thinking of the population, much of it young, that suffers most from this isolation. It still behooves us to use restraint and to look for ways to forestall future miscalculations like the ones we have seen in the past.

NORTH KOREA'S REAL PROBLEM: REGULATING CHANGE

North Korea is a bit smaller, and more mountainous, than South Korea. Its central area is in high mountains that experience cruel winters so that its population of twenty-three million is strung out along the eastern coast and in broad valleys of the west. It is often said that North Korea was Korea's industrial half, with rushing rivers for hydroelectric power and rich deposits of minerals along with extensive forests for timber. When Japan ruled Korea (1910–45) it built ports and railroads and industrial facilities in the northeast, creating an industrial flow that ran from Japan across the sea to northeastern Korea and by rail into southern Manchuria, bypassing the agricultural south. This developed industrial zone was a basic staging area for Japan's war with China, which began in 1937.

Japan's development of the Korean northwest was also industrial, especially along the main rail line that ran north from Pusan through Seoul and Pyongyang to the border with Manchuria at Sinŭiju. If Pyongyang was a market and administrative center for the northwest, much of the mineral wealth of northern Korea was extracted and transported via short lengths of rail line down to the main south-north line to be exported to Japan. The food that was grown on the level ground of South P'yŏng'an and Hwanghae Province was also shipped to Japan by rail or through the ports of Haeju and Namp'o.

This pattern of development under Japanese colonial rule created a regional symbiosis between the "industrial north" and the "agricultural south." It is easy to overstate the importance of this binary idea because there was considerable industry in the south and considerable agriculture in the north. However, the interruption of the two regional economies by the division of Korea in 1945 cut Korea in half economically as well as geographically. A well-known demonstration of this happened in May 1948, when the emerging North Korean regime cut off the power to South Korea as part of the North's political protest against the elections that led to the creation of a separate Korean republic in the southern half of the peninsula.

During the Korean War (1950–53), American bombing essentially pulverized the industrial infrastructure that had been built by the Japanese in North Korea. Although Japan had left much industrial wherewithal in North Korea, the U.S. Air Force made short work of the ports and manufacturing centers and settled down to wiping out the north's bridges, roads, and railroads; rolling stock and vehicles; and, above all, the electrical grid, starting with known power plants and the hydroelectric dams along the Yalu River. In the waning months of the war, with nearly nothing left to destroy, the bombers went after the food supply, hitting irrigation dams in hopes of breaking North Korean morale.[3]

After the armistice that ended the Korean War in July 1953, North Korea's communist allies contributed much to the country's reconstruction. This was in part because of the cold war rivalry between East and West, which on the Korean Peninsula created a kind of race between the South and the North to prove which system—capitalist or communist—was more resilient and better able to provide for its people. East Germany, for example, organized the design and provisions for the reconstruction of the port city of Hamhŭng, on the east coast, a city that had been 80 percent destroyed and had lost 90 percent of its living space during the war.[4] Across the board, the Soviet Union and China helped rebuild North Korea's transportation and energy systems, and for decades thereafter North Korea enjoyed a special trading relationship with the entire communist community, which accepted Korean minerals and other raw materials in exchange for strategic commodities such as oil and steel and military equipment to help the North Koreans face the perceived threat from South Korea, the United States, and Japan.

A decade after the end of the Korean War, with the emerging split between the Soviet Union and China over leadership of the communist nations, North Korea under Kim Il-sung undertook a middle course, launching the national policy called *Juch'esŏng*, or *Juch'e* for short. The launch of the *Juch'e* middle way not only meant trying to keep from choosing sides in the Sino-Soviet split but it also required the purging of North Korean Communists who were personally allied with the Chinese or Soviets—for example, Koreans who had fought alongside the Chinese Communists in the Chinese civil war of the late 1940s. Thus *Juch'e* coincided with a series of bloody purges in North Korea by means of which Kim Il-sung eliminated rivals within his own Communist movement.

The Korean term *Juch'e* is hard to translate, but an approximation would be "self-reliance," and when Kim proclaimed it, he said it meant that the DPRK would learn to live without handouts and get used to providing for itself. This meant not incurring further debts of gratitude to bigger communist countries that might try to force North Korea to do things in return. It would surely mean living with less, but at least the Koreans would be taking care of themselves. Today, in the North Korean capital of Pyongyang, there is a giant tower, topped by a torch, called the Tower of the *Juch'e* Idea, which stands as a symbol of the Kim Il-sung's political philosophy.

The DPRK continued to benefit from barter arrangements with other communist countries throughout the 1980s. However, the heavy expenses of maintaining its huge military establishment, the inefficiencies of a centrally controlled command economy, the poverty of North Korea's agricultural land, and bad luck in the form of weather disasters all handicapped North Korea's further growth. What had appeared to be a system that was outrunning the capitalist south in the 1970s slowly fell behind, with deteriorating living standards and shortages of every kind of commodity.

Figure 5.1: Kim Il-sung (*right*) and Kim Jong-il (*left*) represented on the shore of the Lake of Heaven atop Mount Paektu.

In practice, what *Juch'e* has meant to North Korea is the promotion of an "autarkic" system—a system that is closed and does not participate (much) in world trade. *Autarky* is one of the words that describe North Korea. Another is *Stalinist*, a term that relates to Josef Stalin's twisting of the ideas of socialism in revolutionary Russia into what became, in the 1930s, a state cult focused on his own leadership. In Stalinism what matters most is not revolutionary idealism (although that is important) but loyalty to the leader. In North Korea, if a person wants to thrive, the most important thing is to demonstrate loyalty to the country's leadership, formerly in the person of Chairman Kim Jong-il, the heir of the late president Kim Il-sung, and now in the person of the sucessor, Kim Jong-un. This focus on Kim Il-sung, the "Great Leader," who is formally still the president of the DPRK even though he died in 1994, and on Kim's son and grandson, is not communist in the sense that Karl Marx envisioned communism. [5] It is a variant—some would say a corruption—of communism. Perhaps *corporatism* would be a more useful term to describe the North Korean system.

Some observers use the word *corporatist* to describe North Korea. Corporatist systems often see their people and institutions as components of a common "body." Thus, an individual does not have a meaningful existence apart from the body and the role he or she plays in maintaining its health. A Confucian society like that of North Korea can identify with corporatism because of the traditional emphasis on family and family loyalty and the function of the individual within society. In this construction, North Korea is a family, the leaders are parents, and the people have proper places, where they belong and from which they are not entitled to deviate. [6]

North Korea's hybrid of Confucianism, autarky (the *Juch'e* idea), Stalinism (called Kimilsungism in the DPRK), corporatism, and communism is the result of how the country was born and grew as a state. The DPRK started out in 1948 with strong memories of the Korean monarchy (before 1910) and the cult of the Japanese emperor (between 1910 and 1945 but especially during the war years, 1937–45). Both the monarchy and the imperial cult attributed a kind of divinity to the national leader, whether the Korean king or the Japanese emperor. While it is true that Korean communists were always highly nationalistic and anti-Japanese, they inherited established patterns of leadership and citizenship that summoned from the general population an unquestioning loyalty and support for a ruler who was seen as legitimate. During the former royal dynasty (the Chosŏn period that ended in 1910), Confucian ethics

Figure 5.2: Tower of the Juch'e Idea, located across the Taedong River from Kim Il-sung Square, Pyongyang. Photo by Donald Clark.

had upheld the king as an unchallengeable national father supported by loyal government officials. When they ruled Korea, the colonial Japanese pointed to the wartime threat from the West and taught Koreans that the survival of their community required unwavering obedience and loyalty from everyone. Deviation and dissent were luxuries that the system could ill afford. In fact, disagreement was considered more than unpatriotic; it was actually treason, in other words, a crime. While this authoritarian heritage was influential in South Korea as well, especially during the era of military rule (1961–93), South Korea had a larger population and many more influences from the outside to make its society more diverse. The leaders of the more isolated DPRK were better able than those in the south to maintain a single-minded focus on the creation of single mass society.[7]

North Korea's social and political structure thus reflects traditions inherited from the Confucian monarchy and imperial Japan. During the creation of the DPRK as a state, certain kinds of people were identified essentially as enemies of the system. Much more than in the South, the ax fell on "collaborators"—Koreans who had prospered under the Japanese either as landlords or as businessmen. Other groups singled out for persecution included people who were opposed to communism from the beginning, such as Christians. Later on, class enemies came to include people who had helped United Nations forces during the Korean War and members of factions of the Korean Workers Party (the communist party) that were rivals of Kim Il-sung's own faction and were subjected to the purges of the 1950s. Being labeled disloyal to the system meant being deprived of the system's socialist benefits, namely, a guaranteed job and income, housing, food rations, health care, and much else. Since the system assigned people to housing, the best housing in Pyongyang was reserved for government workers and others deemed loyal to the Kimilsungist system.

If these are the "rules of the game" for North Korea, what has been the system's performance over the decades? One recognizes that the North Korean system outperformed South Korea in terms of manufacturing output and living standards for the first two decades following the Korean War, thanks largely to special help from other socialist countries. The emphasis was on heavy industry and infrastructure, not consumer goods, and the overall national output grew at astonishing annual rates ranging from 14 to 25 percent, achieving goals set in a succession of five- and seven-year plans. In the 1970s, reaching for the next developmental level, North Korea started importing new machinery for plants to make steel, petrochemicals, and cement, among other things, and it quickly ran into financing problems. Weaknesses became apparent in energy and transportation, and North Korea was hard pressed to develop technologies for the information age, although it did develop an internal network and manufacture its own computers and software packages. Publicly accessible computers, in fact, are still rare in North Korea.

At the beginning of the 1990s, North Korea suffered a series of very heavy blows. One was the fall of communism in Europe, ending what had been a beneficial trading environment for the DPRK. To add insult to injury, Hungary, Poland, and even China and the Soviet Union started doing business with South Korea over objections from the North. Then the Soviet Union itself collapsed. This had several direct consequences for the DPRK. One was that the new Russian Federation began demanding payment in real money—not bartered raw materials—for goods, mainly oil, that were critical to North Korea. Another was that the mutual defense treaty—the Soviet "nuclear umbrella" that had protected North Korea from American nuclear attack—was canceled, leaving the North without a dependable nuclear deterrent in a neighborhood where China, Russia, and the United States had nuclear weapons. North Korea's other near neighbors, South Korea and Japan, although they did not have nuclear weapons, were heavily invested in electricity generation by means of nuclear plants that could, if need be, be turned to the production of atomic weapons material.

Under these severe stresses, North Korea responded in several apparently contradictory ways, all at the same time. It opened a dialogue with South Korea and agreed to membership in the United Nations for both the DPRK and the ROK. It announced plans to build special economic zones, somewhat similar to the coastal areas that had powered China's entry into the modern world economy, in the far northeast and far northwest. And it undertook to modernize its energy sector by beginning construction on new nuclear power plants, which had the dual capability to produce materials for atomic weapons. This led to the first nuclear confrontation between North Korea and the United States, in 1993–94, in the midst of which Kim Il-sung died. The shock of his death was compounded in the following year by huge storms and floods that destroyed much of North Korea's food production for the year and began a period of famines from which the country has never completely recovered.

The death of President Kim Il-sung in July 1994 hit North Korea as an unprecedented psychological blow. At the time he had been in power longer than any other leader in the world, and most Koreans had never known life without him. Although outsiders predicted a damaging power struggle in Pyongyang, the succession from the father to his son, Kim Jong-il, proceeded with surprising smoothness. After a period in seclusion, appearing to mourn the death of his father in a way suggestive of old Confucian mourning practices under the monarchy, Kim Jong-il emerged as the supreme leader in his own right by 1998. While his leadership certainly was not predictable or even understable from the outside at times, he faced and overcame an impressive series of circumstantial challenges, including the weather disasters of the mid-1990s and the subsequent famine and consequential health and nutrition emergencies that complicated what his people look back upon as their "Arduous March." North Korea watchers often marvel at the way Kim Jong-il maintained his grip on power, often going to the brink of disaster in provocations against South Korea, Japan, the United States, and other international players. The resulting push-back consisted of sanctions which served further to isolate the DPRK and to limit its chances of becoming part of the world economy. Despite fitful episodes of diplomatic contact and even cooperation that led at one point, for example, to dismantling part of the Yongbyon nuclear plant, North Korea under Kim Jong-il remained more of a pariah state than it was under his father. In 2012 the question is whether this situation has to continue under Kim Jong-un and his circle of supporters, or whether the North Korean leadership will look for ways to risk opening and restructuring the system. Optimists on this question have very little to support their point of view, though change of some sort is likely.

North Korea is bordered on the south by the ROK, whose economic output is more than thirty times that of the DPRK and whose standard of living and material comfort are incomparably better. The tightly sealed boundary along the DMZ protects North Korea from the obvious attractions of South Korea to a large extent. However, information does get through. Added to this, on the northern boundary, the Chinese industrial city of Dandong, across the Yalu River from Sinŭiju in the northwest, and the relatively prosperous region of Jiandao in the northeast, are dramatic proof to North Koreans that there are better ways to live. Although the Kim regime in Pyongyang insists that the people of North Korea live in a paradise where they have no reason to envy anyone anywhere in the world, the better life being lived in China, at least, is a fact that surely filters through. The fact is that thousands of North Koreans travel outside the DPRK every year, and thousands of outsiders enter. It is likely, therefore, that somewhere underneath the surface in North Korea there is a lively trade in information about the outside world, with significant ramifications for the survival of the government, which, after all, has been lying for generations to its own people.

Categories of North Koreans who routinely travel outside their country include diplomats and other government officials, persons in charge of trade and other state and private business organizations, students, athletes, performers, airline employees, ships' crews, military personnel, and even tourists from the inner circle of Kim regime loyalists. When North Koreans depart, they usually leave behind family members whose presence in North Korea amounts to a guarantee that the traveler will return. Many "defectors" live with the lives of their relatives on their consciences— whatever form the punishment, if any, may have taken place.

Categories of outsiders who routinely enter North Korea include Korean-speaking family members from the south, Koreans living in China, Korean residents of Japan, ethnic Koreans from all over the world who hold foreign passports including the United States, United Nations officials, diplomats from nations with embassies in the DPRK, humanitarian workers from nongovernmental organizations, businessmen and potential investors, athletes, students, tourists, and performers such as members of the New York Philharmonic Orchestra, which visited Pyongyang in February 2008.

Figure 5.3: Mural of Kim Il-sung visiting workers in Pyongyang's Puhǔng (Revitalization) Metro station. Photo by Donald Clark.

Worldwide, there are many reports about the human rights violations, harsh living conditions, and daily miseries experienced by the people of North Korea, and a brief search on the Internet will turn up quite a number. Many of these reports originate in the accounts of refugees and people who may have an interest in painting the grimmest possible picture of life in the DPRK. However, even the most casual visitor to Pyongyang, which is the best of North Korea, can see conditions that are primitive by comparison with those in South Korea or China. Examples include regular power blackouts that stall streetcars during rush hour, people climbing stairs in high-rise apartment buildings that lack elevators, the lack of heat in the winter and air conditioning in the summer, the relative rarity of computers and telephones, and the bare shelves in stores. If ease is a measure of the quality of life, there is no concealing the fact that North Koreans do not have it easy.

The harshness of life in North Korea and the intentional abuse of certain citizens by the state are topics regularly exposed in the international press. Human Rights Watch, for example, expresses it this way.

> There is no organized political opposition, free media, functioning civil society, or religious freedom. Arbitrary arrest,

detention, and torture and ill-treatment of detainees, and lack of due process remain serious issues. North Korea operates detention facilities including those popularly known as "political prison camps" where hundreds of thousands of its citizens—including children—are enslaved in deplorable conditions for various anti-state offenses. Collective punishment is the norm for such crimes. Periodically, the government publicly executes citizens for stealing state property, hoarding food, and other "anti-socialist" crimes.[8]

This bleak assessment raises questions about whether North Korea is stable enough to survive as a system, since it implies that if controls were ever to be loosened a formidable current of resentment and even revolution would begin to flow. Even if only part of the report's language is entirely accurate, it is easy to see how much the beneficiaries of the present system in North Korea must be committed to preventing change. All our experience suggests that the situation as it is cannot long continue, even though year after year it seems to do just that.

The dilemma for the North Korean state system, therefore, is how to manage the inevitable flow of information into the system and the rising expectations that come—and are coming—with the gradual importation of goods and ideas from the outside. In the Soviet Union, "reform" (referred to as "glasnost," "perestroika," or "restructuring") led to an uncontrollable tide of change that swept the Communist Party out of power. In China, the Chinese Communist Party has managed to enable private market behavior and induce international investments in a fast-growing world economy without relinquishing its monopoly on political power. In the Socialist Republic of Vietnam, something similar is under way. But Pyongyang cannot seem to find a way to follow their examples.

For one thing, neither China nor Vietnam confronts what it sees as a mortal military threat, a problem that requires constant vigilance and a primary emphasis on national defense. As the North Korean system sees it, the "Great General" Kim Jong-il has as his main task the deterrence of attack from the outside, requiring an "Army First" policy that siphons the best of the system's resources into the military. Defense requirements drive the country to resort to varieties of asymmetrical warfare, including the pursuit of a nuclear deterrent and the DPRK's reported pursuit of cyberwar capability.

SYSTEM PERFORMANCE AND THE SUCCESSION

Between 2002 and 2005, the Kim Jong-il regime decided to experiment with very limited market reforms (which it called "Industrial Management Improvement Measures" since *reform* is a term the DPRK tries to avoid). These enabled individuals to sell things in small roadside stalls and even to start businesses (often calling them "joint ventures" with government supervisors). Some of these measures merely lifted bans on things that had actually been going on for years in the black market. But some also quickly came to be seen as subversive. People peddled things that they stole from state supplies. People speculated in prices and took advantage of others. Women, who were assigned to state jobs or home duties in the socialist system, spent too much of their time out selling in the market. The already lively market in methamphetamines exploded into a major drug addiction problem. In sum, the "measures" seemed to foster uncontrollable corruption rather than a better life. So the government, starting in 2005, began trying to reimpose restrictions on behavior, forbidding women younger than fifty from appearing in the market, arresting profiteers and drug peddlers, and making public examples of abusers by firing squad. Further measures included the sudden recall of the North Korean currency, the *wŏn*, in 2009 and the issue of a new series of bills, forcing people to turn in their cash on hand in exchange for the new series. The intent was to let people with legitimate stashes of money trade legally for the new currency but to render worthless fortunes being held in ill-gotten cash by speculators and other criminals. The currency reform, though meant to iron out problems in the system, created massive disruptions of its own, including rare public protests, which brought forth an official government apology and a scramble to repair the damage. The top officials most responsible for the currency disaster reportedly were put to death.

The "Great General" Kim Jong-il apparently suffered a stroke in 2008. For many months he appeared in public only rarely, and he seemed seriously weakened. In one of his last appearances on the rostrum at Kim Il-sung Square in Pyongyang he walked along the handrail but had to hold on, and there were other signs of frailty. Thus his provision for the succession of his youngest son, Kim Jong-un, seems in retrospect to have been hurried, with no time to provide the heir-apparent with anything like the practical political training that he himself acquired during twenty years as his father's understudy. There was no concealing the shock, therefore, when the news announcers came on the television on December 19, 2011 to announce the Great General's sudden death. It took two days for the government to make the announcement, during which time there were doubtless many anguished maneuvers within the ruling circle. Certainly many mysteries shroud the machinations of the political and military elites of the DPRK. But the senior leaders of the Korean Workers Party and the Korean People's Army, and the apparatchiks that support them in the bureaucracy, surely realize that stability is their best choice for the foreseeable future. Their own safety for the time being will require that they quell their impulses to jockey for advantage in the wake of the "Great General's" passing.

The fitness for leadership of Kim Jong-un naturally is a central question. He is the youngest of Kim Jong-il's sons, the offspring of the Great General's late wife Ko Yŏng-hi. He is thought to have attended school in Switzerland for a time during his boyhood, and possibly he speaks some German or English. He did not establish a reputation as a party official-in-training and as recently as April 2010, and he was so little-known that the international media were publishing photos of him that turned out to be of someone else. Kim Jong-un was confirmed as a *taejang*, equivalent to a four-star general, in the Korean People's Army during the Workers' Party Congress in September 2010, a clear sign at the time that he was being positioned for the succession. At the same time his aunt Kim Kyŏng-hŭi, Kim Jong-il's younger sister, was assigned the same army rank, in a way that positioned her and her husband Chang Sŏng-t'aek, as potential protectors of Kim Jong-un in his future position as commander-in-chief. The North Korean shelling of Yŏn'p'yong Island in November 2010 was widely rumored to have been the young Kim's debut as a military adventurer, but instead North Korea ascribed it to orders from Kim Jong-il himself. The fact is that as of the time of Kim Jong-il's death, nobody outside the system seems to have had any clue about what kind of a leader the younger Kim might be—or want to be.

In the elaborate mourning rituals that surrounded the state funeral for Kim Jong-il, much of the North Korean system was on display for analysis by the rest of the world. Though Pyongyang is the DPRK's showcase city, even light dustings of December snow could not conceal the meagerness of life in the capital. Kim Jong'il's posthumous benevolence was demonstrated by special rations of dried fish, distributed by dour shopgirls in freezing stores to long lines of sorrowing housewives. Along the streets, Kim's cortege was greeted by ranks of thousands of tearful citizens, some of them acting under peer pressure no doubt but many more frightened and unsettled at the thought of a DPRK perhaps defenseless without the leadership of the Great General.

Even so, notwithstanding Western press speculation that North Korea at long last was free to collapse, it seemed that the control mechanisms were doing their work and that the succession, sudden though it was, was proceeding in an orderly way that would guarantee at least the continued powers and privileges of the ruling elites of party and army. Kim Jong-un was swiftly confirmed as Vice-Chairman of the Central Military Commission, a place-holder position that put him at the apex of the leadership without arrogating to himself his father's title as Chairman. Beneath and beside him in the highest councils were army generals and party operatives who were supporters of his father and presumably reliable as supporters of his father's designated successor.

For other key leaders, North Korea watchers studied the rosters of the "funeral committee," long an indicator of who's who in any Communist system, for signs of promotion and demotion. There was, as always, little satisfaction in this exercise. The DPRK is a black box for the intelligence community. No satellites orbiting overhead can see into the minds of the leaders of North Korea; and so we continue to rely on observations of short-term visitors, broken-hearted refugees and angry defectors, South Korean right-wingers with axes to grind, and the fitful attentions of Western journalists and "experts" to predict what will happen next.

A monarchic succession by a third generation is unique in a socialist state. However, taken in North Korean terms as an affirmation of the legitimacy of the Kim family as leaders, it fits a pattern and is not entirely surprising. Kim Jong-un is the genetic material of the Kim cult, the pivot around which the ruling elites of the DPRK now turn. The focus is not on his legitimacy but on his ability to control the rivals in the class that depends on him for survival. For if it is true that the people of North Korea really did revere Kim Jong-il, they cannot have enjoyed the consequences of their government's maladministration. And though in many ways North Korea confounds the lessons of history by its stubborn refusals to collapse, its impenetrable secrets, its cruel corporatist organization, and its popular support for undeserving leaders, everything continues to suggest that it cannot forever remain that way.

In North Korea, therefore, we continue to look for small signs of improvement and rising expectations, remembering that revolutions rarely come from people who are completely without hope. Recent visitors report some signs of improvement in goods available for purchase in the market, construction projects, more vehicles, the widening use of electronic gadgets and cell phones, and other accoutrements of modern life. On the farms also, improvements show in the presence of wild birds, poultry, farm animals, and other protein on the hoof; the use of vinyl on the ground to lengthen the growing season; and trees growing on hillsides without being cut down for fuel. In the western provinces at least, there are few signs of malnutrition or starvation, and people dress reasonably well. On market days there are thriving exchanges in county towns with goods being carried to villages for independent resale at roadside stands. On the other hand, most places still enjoy electric power for only a few hours each day, the transport system is badly broken and poorly maintained (including vehicles, roads, and bridges). Much is still done by hand labor. Although Pyongyang looks dramatically better than other places, with beautiful stadiums and civic centers, ordinary buildings everywhere in the capital show clear signs of age and poor maintenance.[9]

The closed system of the DPRK, the costs of corruption, and the disorganized approach to economic reform, together with the fear of reprisals against deviation of any kind, make it hard to envision a path for North Korea from the place where it now is to the place it needs to be if its people are to have a better life. Although the system is durable and unlikely to collapse, it is hard to chart not only the succession that is now upon them, but also the kind of transition that would be required if the people of North Korea were to leave behind their broken autarky and reach for a role in the world economy. With the succession of the untested Kim Jong-un as supreme leader, the Kimilsungist regime in Pyongyang continues to rely on memories of the "Great Sun of the Twenty-first Century, our General Kim Jong-il" and fidelity to the sacred creed of *Juch'e* to buy a little more time. One can only hope that North Korea's new ruling circle will use the time to find a way to change without bringing on more human suffering in a nation that has endured altogether too much social and economic trouble.

6

Thinking About the
Future of Korea

The Problem of Reunification

Since the end of the Korean War, the problem of reunification has always been uppermost on the Korean agenda. Most Koreans claim to yearn for national reunification. However, the opposing systems in North and South Korea are incompatible, and reunification almost certainly would mean destruction of one in favor of the other. Since the military establishments and economic elites on both sides benefit from the systems existing as they now do, many questions arise about how reunification could be effected without unacceptable costs and disruptions. This is an awkward, even tragic, question, but one that has to be addressed by anyone seriously contemplating a reunification or reintegration of the two Korean systems.

Many scenarios for Korean reunification have been proposed over the years. One that is continually predicted but never seems to happen is a North Korean system collapse and absorption by South Korea. This "hard landing" for North Korea is fondly desired by conservatives in South Korea, Japan, and the United States, but ever since the reunification of Germany and the attendant costs and difficulties of that national project, South Koreans have soberly reflected on whether their system could stand the financial, political, and social strain of a complete defeat of North Korea.

Another scenario is a "confederation" in which both sides retain some aspects of their differing systems, the way Hong Kong differs from the People's Republic of China. A third scenario, which was tried between 1998 and 2008, is the "Sunshine Policy" (see below), which maintains defenses but patiently tries to engage North Korea. And a fourth scenario is military, also already tried with disastrous results in 1950–53 but occasionally contemplated by people in moments of extreme frustration.

Over the decades, well-meaning efforts to mediate the disputes between North and South have resulted in very little. The two halves of Korea remain divided, mutually antagonistic, and heavily armed for a possible renewal of the war.

One pattern in negotiations between North and South Korea involves proposals that are put forward with the expectation that one side will say no, thus making it possible to blame the other side for blocking reunification. An example would be demanding an admission and apology for some alleged misdeed as a precondition for progress in reunification talks. Many talks between North and South have thus been mere shouting matches. This pattern is no accident. A major reason for the existence of both governments is national security, and the ceaseless recriminations make it obvious that the two sides have to maintain their vigilant military postures. The powers that be in Seoul and Pyongyang are thus affirmed in their power, although the relationship between them is mostly stuck in paralysis.

Notwithstanding this dreary pattern, one can detect progress toward reunification, or at least reintegration, albeit at a glacial pace. On balance there is increasing trade between the two Koreas. On balance South Korean companies are investing more in North Korea, and there is more human contact between people on both sides. Officials from both sides talk to each other and have even developed relationships. However, North Korean leaders know very well that what is most desired by South Korea and its allies in America and Japan is the extinction of the DPRK. They are therefore resistant to reform proposals because they know that underneath is the intention to cause the extinction of their system. They know that this is a life-and-death matter for them, from watching Eastern Europe and the fate of leaders like Romania's Nicolae Ceauşcescu.

There are better approaches to the problem of Korean reunification or reintegration. Because the North Korean system draws so much of its legitimacy and popular support from the idea that the DPRK is under mortal threat—as in fact it is, judging by the years of threats by South Korean, American, and Japanese leaders—a better approach might be to seek ways to convince the North Koreans that "reforms" will not mean their extinction but instead would mean a chance to preserve what they want to preserve but under better circumstances.

This conceptual framework was behind South Korea's Sunshine Policy, which was launched by President Kim Dae-jung in the late 1990s. The Sunshine Policy resolved to defend South Korea as always but also to

Figure 6.1: South Korean President Kim Dae-jung and North Korean Chairman Kim Jong-il, 2000.

pursue a second track of contacts, investments, visits when possible, and diplomatic coaxing of North Korea into a healthier relationship with the outside world. Initiatives under the Sunshine Policy included an opening for South Korean tourists to visit limited areas of the Diamond Mountains along North Korea's east coast, incentives for South Korean industries to invest in factories located in the north, and an end to hostile rhetoric and verbal attacks on the northern system and its leaders. In June of 2000, Kim Dae-jung made a historic visit to Pyongyang, the first South Korean leader to cross into the DPRK, where he shook hands with Chairman Kim Jong-il and worked out a communiqué full of conciliatory expressions. At the time, Kim Dae-jung's visit to North Korea was regarded as something of a breakthrough, and he was recognized the next year with the Nobel Peace Prize. Some of the dazzle of his success was lost, however, when it turned out that South Korea had donated upward of five hundred million dollars to the North in order to make the visit happen. Many South Korean critics called it a bribe purporting to be a diplomatic accomplishment. It was both.

The Sunshine Policy was an experiment, a new approach to a problem that seemed frozen in impossibility. Kim Dae-jung's determined pursuit of the policy was a sharp departure from the policies of his predecessors, and it is hard to see how any of them could have managed it, both because tensions were higher during earlier decades and because Kim himself had a unique standing as a transcendent politician, sometimes referred to as Korea's Nelson Mandela. He also launched the policy at a moment when his conservative critics were in an unusually weak position during the "IMF crisis" of 1997–99, which shook and somewhat discredited Korea's right-wing establishment.

South Korea's conservative opposition did not stay quiet for long. The Sunshine Policy stirred worries about national security and brought accusations of naïveté about North Korean intentions. In 2001 the new George W. Bush administration in Washington took the same position, openly criticizing the Sunshine Policy and opening a rift with Kim Dae-jung's administration. There was a domestic political reason for this. American neoconservatives were aggressively pursuing "National Missile Defense" at the time and found it useful to cast North Korea as an aggressive threat to its neighbors and the entire world. Bush named North Korea as part of the "Axis of Evil" in his 2002 State of the Union speech, accused it of cheating on its international promises to curb its nuclear program later in that year, and put U.S.–North Korean relations into a deep freeze. The United States then dictated a framework for talking with North Korea that required the presence and concurrence of "six parties"—the United States, South and North Korea, Japan, China, and Russia—before anything could be accomplished. Given the differing interests of the parties, the "Six Party Talks," made little headway. North Korea remained a pariah state, and, although Kim Dae-jung's successor, President Roh Moo-hyun, continued the Sunshine Policy after 2003, he faced heavy going against internal opponents and the Bush administration.

The Sunshine Policy ended after the presidential terms of Kim Dae-jung and Roh Moo-hyun, becoming essentially a dead letter—a failed experiment—by 2008, with the inauguration of a new conservative administration in South Korea under President Lee Myung-bak. The widespread conclusion in South Korea was that the Kim and Roh administrations had given too much to the North and received too little in return. The North Koreans' conclusion seemed to be that regardless of the momentary leanings of the Kim and Roh administrations, the South Korean establishment remained implacably anti-DPRK, the United States was all too determined to see "regime change" in Pyongyang, and the wiser course lay in keeping up their guard.

Certain legacies of the Sunshine Policy remain, and these may be the starting point for future progress toward reconciliation. There are South Korean factories in North Korea, notably a cluster of manufacturing plants that use North Korean labor in a special economic zone at the edge of the DMZ, near the North Korean city of Kaesŏng. South Koreans visit North Korean tourist sites near the border, and a few get visas to do business in the North. A railroad link has been created, and trains have made test runs across the border in both directions, demonstrating the possibility of through transportation between the whole Korean Peninsula and the rail systems of China, Russia, and Western Europe. There have been many family members' visits back and forth, and under the radar thousands of North Korean refugees have found ways across the border to migrate to new lives in South Korea, where they face formidable adjustment problems learning to survive without socialism.

The ascension of Lee Myung-bak to power in South Korea, backed by a conservative press and military establishment, led to much harsher rhetoric against North Korea and a certain amount of posturing on both sides, which aggravated tensions on the Korean Peninsula after 2008. There were serious border clashes, particularly along the sea boundaries between the territorial waters of the two sides. The most serious of these was the sinking in March 2010 of the South Korean corvette *Cheonan* with the loss of forty-six sailors, apparently the result of an exploding North Korean torpedo. Repercussions from this incident included the end most trade and exchanges between North and South and a frightening rise in saber rattling. South Korea and the United States conducted several military exercises designed to intimidate and deter the North—although they also served to underline the fact that the U.S.–South Korean alliance was really in no position to take military action to punish the North, even for sinking a South Korean ship, because of the population concentration on the Korean Peninsula and the risk of massive human casualties in any such attempt. Instead, when the dust settled, the parties went to the United Nations to seek stern language in resolutions condemning North Korea. The U.N. Security Council, under Chinese and Russian influence, watered down the suggested language, and the international community did little more than offer a slap on the wrist.

An even more shocking and dangerous situation erupted in November 2010 when South Korean forces on the island of Yŏn'p'yŏng (also spelled Yeonpyeong) fired practice rounds of artillery in waters contested by the North Koreans. Yŏn'p'yŏng is one of several islands within sight of North Korea just off the west coast. These islands were in United Nations hands when the armistice was signed in 1953 and they have remained under South Korean control ever since. The ROK maintains military bases on the islands and has successfully asserted free access to them from South

Korea. South and North Korea both value the surrounding waters for their rich marine life, including shellfish, and boats from both sides are accustomed to passing in close proximity.

Control of the islands and surrounding waters is contested, however, because the ROK draws a "Northern Limit Line" (NLL) to the north of them, claiming them as South Korean territory subject to South Korean military defense. The DPRK draws a different line, from the emergence of the Military Demarcation Line (MDL), or 1953 truce line, straight west into the Yellow Sea, a line that passes to the south of the islands and fishing grounds and includes them in North Korea's jurisdiction. Although the North Koreans regularly protest South Korean control of the islands and the waters in the contested area, they have rarely taken direct action to challenge or dislodge the forces of the ROK. However, the contested area is a dangerous place to hold military maneuvers, since the other side certainly views them as a challenge. Naval exercises or artillery practice by the South Koreans in the area are regarded by the DPRK as provocations. Indeed, the earlier *Cheonan* incident happened in this area, directly south of one of the islands, and its sinking most likely was related to the ongoing dispute over territorial control.

The occasion for the incident in November 2010 was the South's insistence on its right to engage in artillery practice from Yŏn'p'yŏng Island , aiming at targets that were away from North Korea but which still lay within the contested zone which the North, like the South, claims as territorial waters. When the southern side fired its weapons at the targets, insisting that the operation was taking place entirely south of the "Northern Limit Line," DPRK shore batteries fired on Yŏn'p'yŏng Island, killing two ROK Marines and two civilians and wounding sixteen others. This was generally seen as the most dangerous outbreak of violence between the two sides since the end of the Korean War in 1953, and it required great restraint by both sides to prevent escalation into something even more serious. At the conclusion of the incident, the ROK side declared that it would no longer bind itself to "proportional responses" against North Korean military actions, meaning that instead of just returning artillery fire as they did in November 2010, if any such incident were to occur in the future, the southern side would retaliate with more force—presumably to include air attacks on North Korean territory.

The Yŏn'p'yŏng Island bombardment demonstrated once more the fragility of the security situation on the Korean peninsula. Long-time observers were shocked at the suddenness with which the situation deteriorated from normal to critically dangerous—just hours from a peaceful situation to the brink of all-out war that could have embroiled allies on both sides such as the United States and China. Fortunately, the parties on all sides were able to back away in a formidable trial of patience, recognizing that the only sane choice was restraint.

Something to hope for in the future is better coordination in a confident but conciliatory stance by the U.S.-ROK-Japanese alliance in a policy that reassures the North Koreans even while encouraging conditions for change in their system. North Korea wants a peace treaty with the United States and a chance to deal with America on an "equal" basis, meaning diplomatic relations and some level of access to foreign aid and the benefits of participation in the world trading system. The United States is invested in a framework of talks among six nations—the United States, China, Russia, Japan, and the two Koreas—to "solve" the Korean "problem," including the urgent problem of nuclear proliferation by the DPRK and the export of weapons, including exports to terrorists. Over the years, a means of reconciling these two positions has emerged, whereby U.S. and North Korean representatives talk "within the context of the Six Party Talks." Indeed, near the end of 2011, the United States was about to resume humanitarian aid to North Korea and to answer North Korea's invitation to resume the Six Party Talks when Kim Jong-il suddenly died in December.

Kim's death presented at least one interesting opportunity for a changed mode of communication with North Korea. Though hard-liners in both countries objected vigorously, South Korea and the United States avoided celebratory language or statements that insulted the memory of the North Korean leader. The South Koreans went farther than the Americans, who simply expressed hope for new opportunities. Seoul expressed sympathy with the people of North Korea without directly expressing condolences or sorrow at the death of Kim Jong-il. This was in contrast to "good riddance"-type statements that had come from South Korean leaders in 1994 following the death of the DPRK founder Kim Il-sung.

Some observers regretted the lost opportunity to do more, however. Seoul did not send an official delegation: the most senior South Korean visitors to Pyongyang were the widow of former President Kim Dae-jung and the chairwoman of the Hyundai Group, whose father was long identified with the unification issue. North Korea criticized South Korea for holding back, but this time at least no bridges were burned between them.

All sides are prisoners, to some degree, of things they have said in the past about what they would and would not do. It would be useful to be able to leave that baggage behind and look for more flexibility. Much "face" is involved, of course, but this is normal. Real negotiation is about finding ways for the other side to say yes without losing face. The issues are complicated and progress is maddeningly slow. But year by year there are more and more signs of common ground and reasons to hope that the people of Korea, on both sides of their tragic dividing line, can find ways to make their broken country whole again.

NOTES

CHAPTER 1

[1] Basic facts about South and North Korea can be found in the *CIA World Fact Book* online at https://www.cia.gov/library/publications/the-world-factbook

[2] Among the best short introductions to the history of Korean Americans are Nancy Abelmann and John Lie, *Blue Dreams: Korean Americans and the Los Angeles Riots* (Cambridge: Harvard University Press, 1995), chap. 3; and Eui-young Yu, "The Korean-American Community," in *Korea Briefing, 1993*, ed. Donald N. Clark, 139–62 (Boulder: Westview Press, 1993).

[3] "The Role of Korean American Churches in the Twenty-first Century" is the title of a collection of articles that examines the place and function of Korean churches in the history of the Korean American community. See *Korean and Korean American Studies Bulletin*, special issue, 17, nos. 1–2 (2009).

[4] See Abelmann and Lie, *Blue Dreams*, especially chapters 3, 4, and 5.

[5] Pak Taehŏn, *Sŏyangini pon Chosŏn: Chosŏn kwan'gye sŏyang sŏji* (Korea as Seen by Westerners: Western Books on Korea, 1655–1949), vol. 1 (Seoul: Sosanbang Rare Books, 1996), 16.

CHAPTER 2

[1] For regional Korean food specialties, see Michael Pettid, *Korean Cuisine: An Illustrated History* (London: Reaktion Books, 2008), 91–109.

[2] The story of Tan'gun, as told by the monk Iryŏn in his *Samguk Yusa* (Memorabilia of the Three Kingdoms), is translated in Peter H. Lee and William Theodore DeBary, eds., *Sources of Korean Tradition*, vol. 1: *From Early Times through the Sixteenth Century* (New York: Columbia University Press, 1997), 5–6.

[3] See Sarah Milledge Nelson, *The Archaeology of Korea* (Cambridge: Cambridge University Press, 1993), especially chapter 4.

[4] The standard work on Paekche in English is Jonathan Best, *A History of the Early Korean Kingdom of Paekche, Together with an Annotated Translation of the Paekche Annals of the Samguk Sagi* (Cambridge: Harvard University Press, 2007). To be sure, many Korean art treasures now in Japan representing Paekche and other eras of Korean history were simply taken there over the centuries, most notably during the colonial period when Japan ruled Korea (1910–45).

[5] For a thoughtful discussion of the meaning of Silla in modern Korean life and the way the city has been reconstructed (and largely reimagined), see Robert Oppenheim, *Kyŏngju Things: Assembling Places* (Ann Arbor: University of Michigan Press, 2008).

[6] See Edward J. Shultz, *Generals and Scholars: Military Men in Medieval Korea* (Honolulu: University of Hawai'i Press, 2000).

[7] See John B. Duncan, *The Origins of the Chosŏn Dynasty* (Seattle: University of Washington Press, 2000).

[8] See William R. Shaw, *Legal Norms in a Confucian State* (Berkeley: University of California Press, 1981), 99–106; and Lee and DeBary, *Sources of Korean Tradition*, 558–71.

[9] For King Sejong see Young-Key Kim Renaud, ed., *King Sejong the Great* (Washington, D.C.: International Circle of Korean Linguistics, 1992).

[10] The pioneering work on this is Edward W. Wagner, *The Literati Purges: Political Conflict in Early Yi Korea* (Cambridge: Harvard University Press, 1974).

[11] One of these accounts was the *Hanjung-nok*, translated by Jahyun Kim Haboush as *The Memoirs of Lady Hyegyŏng: The Autobiographical Writings of a Crown Princess of Eighteenth Century Korea* (New York: Columbia University Press, 1996).

[12] See Hyung-il Pai, *Constructing "Korean" Origins: A Critical Review of Archaeology, Historiography, and Racial Myth in Korean State Formation Theories* (Cambridge: Harvard University Press, 2000).

[13] For a study of how the Korean official class dealt with change after the Japanese and Manchu invasions, see James B. Palais, *Confucian Statecraft and Korean Institutions: Yu Hyŏngwŏn and the Late Chosŏn Dynasty* (Seattle: University of Washington Press, 1996). For the social and regional dynamics of change in the late Chosŏn period, see Kyung Moon Hwang, *Beyond Birth: Social Status in the Emergence of Modern Korea* (Cambridge: Harvard University Asia Center, 2004). For the conservative ruling class's response to pressure from the outside, see Martina Deuchler, *Barbarian Envoys and Confucian Gentlemen: The Opening of Korea, 1875–1885* (Seattle: University of Washington Press, 1977).

[14] Don Baker, "A Different Thread: Orthodoxy, Heterodoxy, and Catholicism in a Confucian World," in *Culture and the State in Late Chosŏn Korea*, ed. Jahyun Kim Haboush and Martina Deuchler, 199–232 (Cambridge: Harvard University Asia Center, 1999).

[15] Sun Joo Kim, *Marginality and Subversion in Korea: The Hong Kyŏngnae Rebellion of 1812* (Seattle: University of Washington Press, 2007).

[16] The many-faceted process by which Korea was set adrift from the Chinese tributary system and eventually subjected to Japanese colonial domination is the subject of many books and studies. A classic account employing

Japanese sources is Hillary Conroy, *The Japanese Seizure of Korea: A Study of Realism and Idealism in International Relations* (Philadelphia: University of Pennsylvania Press, 1960). It was answered from the side of Korean scholars by C. I. Eugene Kim and Han-kyo Kim, *Korea and the Politics of Imperialism, 1876–1910* (Berkeley: University of California Press, 1967). Andre Schmid, *Korea between Empires, 1895–1919* (New York: Columbia University Press, 2002), tracks the evolution of Korean reform thought; Vipan Chandra, *Imperialism, Resistance, and Reform in Late Nineteenth-Century Korea* (Berkeley: University of California Press, 1988), in particular follows the Independence Club, a collection of Western-oriented Korean reformers at the turn of the century; and Alexis Dudden, *Japan's Colonization of Korea: Discourse and Power* (Honolulu: University of Hawai'i Press, 2005), is a study of the way Japan used international law and power politics to justify its conquest of Korea.

CHAPTER 3

[1] Edwin H. Gragert, *Landownership under Colonial Rule: The Korean Experience, 1910–1935* (Honolulu: University of Hawai'i Press, 1994), especially chapters 4, 5, and 6.

[2] Michael Edson Robinson, *Cultural Nationalism in Colonial Korea, 1920–1925* (Seattle: University of Washington Press, 1988).

[3] Among the best of many published accounts is *True Stories of the Korean Comfort Women*, ed. Keith Howard and trans. Young Joo Lee (London: Cassell, 1995).

CHAPTER 4

[1] For an excellent study of how the Soviet-backed Kim Il-sung regime did away with rival claimants to power or drove them to the point of migrating south, see Adam Cathcart and Charles Kraus, "Peripheral Influence: The Sinŭiju Student Incident of 1945 and the Impact of Soviet Occupation in North Korea," *Journal of Korean Studies* 13, no. 1 (fall 2008): 1–28. The standard monograph on the period is Charles K. Armstrong, *The North Korean Revolution, 1945–1950* (Ithaca: Cornell University Press, 2002).

[2] There are many histories of the Korean War, some better than others. The standard account of its background is Bruce Cumings, *The Origins of the Korean War*, vol. 1: *Liberation and the Emergence of Separate Regimes, 1945–1947* (Princeton: Princeton University Press, 1981); and Bruce Cumings, *The Origins of the Korean War*, vol. 2: *The Roaring of the Cataract, 1947–1950* (Princeton: Princeton University Press, 1990); to which should be added John Merrill, *Korea: The Peninsular Origins of the War* (Newark, Del.: University of Delaware Press, 1980); and Alan R. Millett, *The War for Korea, 1945–50: A House Burning* (Lawrence: University of Kansas Press, 2005).

CHAPTER 5

[1] The "headless beast" characterization of North Korea was on the cover of the July 18, 1994, issue of *Newsweek*, following the unexpected death of President Kim Il-sung. The fiery background of the cover suggested a weird mixture of Greek and Chinese mythologies about out-of-control beasts that needed to be slain—in the case of the Lernean hydra, for example, to be killed, once and for all, by Hercules, who found a way to stop it from regenerating heads whenever it was decapitated.

[2] Variations on this idea are attributed to Carl Von Clausewitz, Helmuth von Moltke, Dwight D. Eisenhower, and Colin Powell among many others.

[3] By 1953 the North Koreans had proven resourceful in taking rapid countermeasures against every kind of American bombing tactic. In May American planners decided to bomb agricultural lands, attacking irrigation dikes, dams, ponds, and canals to create sudden floods. An early bombing of a large dam at Tŏksan, north of Pyongyang, wiped out a five-square-mile area of rice fields. A second bombing of a dike in Chasŏn was also destructive, but subsequent bombings were not as successful. See Robert A. Pape, *Bombing to Win: Air Power and Coercion in War*, Cornell Studies in Security Affairs (Ithaca: Cornell University Press, 1996), 163.

[4] Rüdiger Frank, "The Hamhŭng Project and the Development of GDR-DPRK Relations in the 1950s," paper presented at the annual meeting of the Association for Korean Studies in Europe (AKSE), Prague, 1995; Rüdiger Frank, *Die DDR und Nordkorea: Der Wiederaufbau der Stadt Hamhùng von 1954–1962* (Aachen: Shaker, 1996).

[5] Kim Jong-il is not the president or prime minister of the DPRK. His only formal title is Chairman of the Military Defense Commission. Of course this does not reflect his true position at the pinnacle of the North Korean system. The DPRK press often strings together honorifics. For example, the front page of a newspaper might carry a story that reads, "The respected leader of our party and people, the General Secretary of the Korean Workers Party and Chairman of the National Defense Commission of the Democratic People's Republic of Korea, the Honorable Comrade Kim Jong-il, recently attended a concert at the Mansudae Arts Hall." This one is quoted from *Rodong Sinmun* (Pyongyang), April 4, 2010, 1.

[6] For a good précis of corporatism as it applies to North Korea, see Bruce Cumings, *Korea's Place in the Sun* (New York: W. W. Norton, 2005), 398–402.

[7] There is some controversy over how much weight to give Korea's monarchic traditions and imperial Japan's modern influence on the development of the DPRK. B. R. Myers, for example, concedes that the political impulses of imperial Japan may be visible in the North Korean system, but he suggests that Confucianism, contrary to the interpretations of many other writers, is far in the background. See B. R. Myers, *The Cleanest Race: How North Koreans See Themselves—and Why It Matters* (Brooklyn: Melville House, 2010), especially chapter 3.

[8] "Human Rights Watch: Events of 2009," http://www.hrw.org/en/node/87398

[9] These remarks are based on the author's observations during a trip through Pyongyang and North and South Hwanghae Provinces in March–April 2010.

GLOSSARY

Chaebŏl: A conglomerate of companies, usually owned by one family or a small group of investors. *Chaebŏl* conglomerates may have their own manufacturing, construction, trading, and financial components. Leading *chaebŏl* include Hyundai, Samsung, the LG Group, and Daewoo. Smaller *chaebŏl* such as Hanjin and Kumho specialize in transportation, running airlines (Korean Air and Asiana), and Hanjin container freight shipping.

Chang Sŏng-t'aek (Jang Song-thaek). (1946–): Vice-Chairman of the National Defense Commission of the DPRK, North Korea's most important decision-making body. A long-time party operative, husband of Kim Il-sung's daughter Kim Kyŏng-hŭi and supporter of Kim Jong-il, he was demoted in 2004 and reinstated in 2009 next to Kim Jong-il in the NDC. Reportedly the second most-powerful person in North Korea after Kim Jong-il's death, essentially a regent for the successor Kim Jong-un. With a party (not army) background, he was noticeably wearing an army uniform during photographs of mourning for Kim Jong-il.

Chosŏn: An ancient name for Korea, derived from Chinese. Also the name of the last royal dynasty (1392–1910). Although South Korea uses the term *Han'guk* for "Korea," the term *Chosŏn* is still in use in the North.

Chun Doo-hwan (Chŏn Tuhwan). (1931–): South Korean army general who seized power in 1980 and served as president of the Republic of Korea from 1980 to 1988.

Comfort women: Female conscript laborers from Korea and other countries who were used as sex slaves by the Japanese military forces during World War Two.

Demilitarized Zone (DMZ): Established by the 1953 armistice agreement that ended the fighting in the Korean War, the DMZ is a strip of land extending across the Korean Peninsula that separates the forces of South Korea and the United Nations Command in the South and

North Korean forces in the North. The DMZ is 248 kilometers long and 4 kilometers wide, with a line exactly in the middle called the Military Demarcation Line (MDL). Although there are many fortifications in and around the DMZ, it has been largely undisturbed since the Korean War and has developed into something of a wildlife refuge, especially for migratory birds.

Democratic People's Republic of Korea (DPRK): Established in 1948, the DPRK is the northern part of the Korean Peninsula under the governing control of the communist Korean Workers Party (KWP) led by Kim Il-sung (1912–94) and his son Kim Jong-il (1942–).

Han'gŭl: Korean term for the phonetic alphabet presented to the people in 1446 by King Sejong of the Chosŏn dynasty.

Juch'e (chuch'e): The "self-reliance" philosophy that is central to the political ideology of North Korea and the theoretical basis of the Kim Il-sung cult (Kimilsungism). Originally articulated by Kim Il-sung to assert North Korea's neutrality, or independence, during the years of the Sino-Soviet split, devotion to the *juch'e* idea today is the principle that underlies the country's reluctance to open its doors to foreign influences.

Kim Dae-jung (Kim Taejung). (1939–2009): President of the Republic of Korea (South Korea), elected in 1997. Originally from Korea's southwest, as a national assemblyman Kim Dae-jung ran for president against Park Chung-hee in 1971 and did surprisingly well, winning 45.3 percent of the popular vote. Thereafter, as he emerged as a leading critic of the military-led government, he was subjected to heavy political persecution, including house arrest, imprisonment, kidnapping, and attempts on his life. Surviving these, he ran again for president in 1987 and 1992, then won the election in 1997 as the South Korean economy was undergoing a serious collapse. Kim's leadership is credited with creating conditions for the post-1997 recovery and the more conciliatory South Korean attitude toward North Korea known as the Sunshine Policy.

Kim Il-sung (Kim Ilsŏng). (1912–94): Born in Pyongyang during the Japanese colonial period, Kim Il-sung grew up to be an anti-Japanese guerrilla fighter on the Manchurian border and eventually became an officer in an ethnic Korean unit of the Soviet Red Army during World War Two. Soviet authorities installed him as the leader of their occupation zone in northern Korea in 1945, and he emerged as leader of the DPRK when it was founded in 1948. His decision to reunite the

Korean Peninsula by force led to the Korean War (1950–53). After eliminating rivals and challengers after the war, Kim continued to rule in North Korea until his death in 1994. His personality cult became a major motif of the North Korean state, and he lives on as a legend in the political culture of the DPRK.

Kim Jong-il (Kim Chŏng'il). (1942–): Trained by his father, Kim Il-sung, as an operative of the Korean Workers Party, Kim Jong-il emerged in the 1980s as a contender for the succession and was given progressively greater responsibilities in the ruling party. By the early 1990s he was clearly in a position to continue his father's rule in North Korea within the philosophy of Kimilsungism, which provides for a monarchical-type succession in the KWP and national leadership. Though sometimes derided in the West as a lightweight, Kim Jong-il apparently commands the loyalty of the party leadership and of most, if not all, of North Korea's citizens.

Kim Jong-un (Kim Chŏng'ŭn). (1983?–): Third and youngest son of Chairman Kim Jong-il and grandson of DPRK founder Kim Il-sung; assigned the rank of *taejang* (Great General) in the Korean People's Army in 2010; successor to supreme leadership in North Korea upon the death of his father in December 2011; confirmed as Vice-Chairman of the Central Military Commission of the DPRK; unofficially supreme leader of North Korea.

Kim Yŏng-nam. (1928–): Chairman of the Presidium of the Supreme People's Assembly of the DPRK, in effect the chief of state and one of the three or four top leaders of North Korea. Formerly DPRK Foreign Minister

Kimilsungism: Term denoting the belief system in North korea that makes the state's founder, Kim Il-sung (1912–1994) the source of political wisdom and practice in the DPRK. Sometimes likened to a religion or cult, it raises the person of Kim Il-sung to a superhuman status and his *juch'e* idea to the level of absolute truth.

Koguryŏ: Located in southern Manchuria and northern Korea, the state of Koguryŏ was one of the Korean Three Kingdoms with a founding date traditionally set at 37 BCE. In the early seventh century, Koguryŏ forces successfully repelled repeated Chinese attempts to impose their control over Korea. Koguryŏ was finally conquered by the kingdom of Silla in 668 CE.

Koryŏ: The state of Koryŏ (918–1392) was based in the capital city of Kaesŏng north of Seoul. The name Koryŏ is the basis for the national name, Korea.

Kyŏngju: Capital of the kingdom of Silla in southeastern Korea. Now a "museum without walls," the city is famous for its ancient royal tombs and monumental Buddhist art.

Paekche: One of the Korean Three Kingdoms, Paekche was located in the southwestern part of the peninsula between its traditional founding date of 18 BCE and 663 CE. It served as a conduit for continental influence during the period, including the introduction of Buddhism to Japan.

Paektu, Mount (Paektu-san): An extinct volcano in the Ever White (Changpai) Range on the border between northeastern Korea and China, Mount Paektu is a national symbol for the Korean people, reputedly the location of the founding of the Korean race (*minjok*), and supposedly the birthplace of North Korean leader Kim Jong-il. It is more than nine thousand feet high and topped by a caldera that contains a very deep lake called Ch'ŏnji (Lake of Heaven). Mount Paektu is a favorite tourist destination for overseas Koreans, as well as Koreans from the northern and southern republics. The Yalu and Tumen Rivers emerge from its western and eastern slopes, and a third stream eventually joins the Sungari River in Manchuria.

Panmunjŏm: A village on the battle line during the Korean War that was used for cease-fire negotiations and eventually became the site for the signing of the July 1953 armistice, which ended the fighting. Since then, it has become a meeting place for delegations from the Communist side (North Korea and China) and the United Nations side (represented until recently by the United States but also including South Korea). Panmunjŏm is located in the Demilitarized Zone and sometimes serves as a transit point for persons passing across the line that separates North and South Korea.

Park Chung-hee (Pak Chŏnghŭi). (1917–79): A former schoolteacher and army officer during the Japanese colonial period, Park became a general during the Korean War and took power in May 1961 in a military coup that ended more than a decade of civilian rule in South Korea. He presided over the economic development of South Korea in the 1960s and 1970s. Park was an authoritarian ruler who lost patience with the democratic opposition and ended up ruling by decree. He was assassinated by one of his own deputies in October 1979, an event that opened the way to a further decade of military dictatorship under General Chun Doo-hwan.

Pyongyang: Located on a bend of the Taedong River in North Korea, Pyongyang is Korea's oldest major city and has been the capital of the DPRK since 1948.

Rhee, Syngman (Yi Sŭngman, Ri Sŭngman). (1875–1965): Educated at American mission schools in Korea and then in the United States, Syngman Rhee was an important leader of overseas Korean nationalists during the Japanese colonial period, especially in the United States. After returning to a liberated South Korea in 1945, Rhee maneuvered himself into a leading position with apparent American support and won the presidency of the Republic of Korea in 1948. As president during the Korean War and the period of reconstruction in the 1950s, Rhee often resorted to authoritarian methods and was ousted during a student-led people's revolution in the spring of 1960. He died in exile in Hawaii in 1965.

Ri Yŏng-ho (Yi Yŏngho). (1942–): Chief of staff of the Korean People's Army, Standing member of the Political Bureau of the Korean Worker's [Communist] Party.

Seoul: Located on the north bank of the Han River near the Yellow Sea on a site once occupied by a regional capital of the kingdom of Koryŏ (918–1392), Seoul became the capital of Korea's Chosŏn dynasty in 1396. It continued as the Japanese colonial capital city after the fall of Chosŏn in 1910 and became South Korea's postwar capital in 1945, first as the location of the American military government (1945–48) and then as the seat of the Republic of Korea (1948–present).

Shamanism: An ancient belief system of the Koreans related to versions of shamanism in China, Siberia, and Japan whose variants usually involve communication with the world of spirits, including the spirits of the dead, seeking to enlist the spirits' help or to avoid their wrath.

Silla (Shilla): The longest-lived of the Korean Three Kingdoms with a traditional founding date of 57 BCE. Silla conquered its counterparts, Paekche and Koguryŏ, in the seventh century and was the first to rule most of the Korean Peninsula as a unified state. It gave way to the rise of Koryŏ (which was in some respects a revival of ancient Koguryŏ) in

935. The capital of Silla was the ancient city of Kyŏngju in southeastern Korea.

Yalu River: The Yalu rises from springs on the western slope of Mount Paektu, on the Sino-Korean border, and flows westward to the Yellow Sea. It forms part of the boundary between North Korea and the People's Republic of China and is famous as the limit of the United Nations army's advance during the Korean War before the intervention of the Chinese Communists and the reestablishment of communist military control over North Korea.

Yangban: An aristocratic class of landlords and officials, particularly during the Chosŏn dynasty (1392–1910). Usually a term of respect, it can sometimes simply mean "gentleman" as opposed to "commoner." *Yangban* lineages still carry great prestige and are documented in carefully preserved genealogical records. The term "yangban" literally means "two branches," referring to the civil and military branches of personnel in the Korean royal government.

Suggestions for Further Reading

Korea in General

Baker, Don. *Korean Spirituality.* Honolulu: University of Hawai'i Press, 2009. Useful for insights into traditional systems of belief in Korea and how they interact. Good introduction to Korean animism and shamanism; clear concepts and historical development of Korean Buddhism, Confucianism, and Catholic and Protestant Christianity. From the *Dimensions of Asian Spirituality* series.

Cumings, Bruce. *Korea's Place in the Sun.* New York: W. W. Norton, 2005. After a first chapter that deals with premodern history, Cumings deals in depth with modern Korea since 1860. Engagingly written and with interpretative material that adds much to the discussion, its special strengths are the Korean War era, development of the political economy of South Korea, and a survey chapter on North Korea. Includes helpful chapters on the generations of Korean immigrants to the United States and Korea's global environment in the twenty-first century.

Peterson, Mark, and Philip Margulies. *A Brief History of Korea.* New York: Facts on File, 2010. A brisk survey of traditional periods followed by detailed chapters on the twentieth century. Especially useful as teaching tools are the sidebars and boxes, which bring out key ideas, terms, personalities, and historical influences, as well as the appendixes and bibliography.

Pratt, Keith. *Everlasting Flower.* London: Reaktion Books, 2007. A survey text that reflects its author's encyclopedic knowledge of Korean culture, with resources on art, literature, biography, and religion, as well as conventional survey treatments of the main periods, including the modern. An outstanding introduction to Korean civilization.

Fulton, Bruce, and Kwon Young-min. *Modern Korean Fiction: An Anthology.* New York: Columbia University Press, 2005. Fulton and Kwon present a notable range of translated short stories from the 1920s to the late 1990s covering a variety of styles, movements, and periods. A combination of recent writings and retranslations of older canonical works.

Lie, John. *Han Unbound: The Political Economy of South Korea.* Stanford: Stanford University Press, 2000. A rich interweaving of political, social, economic, and even personality factors in the search for a postcolonial development plan, together with a narrative of how South Korea (Han) developed, through many sacrifices and traumas (*han*), from one of the poorest countries on earth into one of the most dynamic and prosperous. Examines the question of whether the story is "uniquely Korean" or transferable as a model elsewhere.

Millett, Allan R. *The War for Korea. Vol. 1: 1945–1950: A House Burning.* Lawrence: University Press of Kansas, 2005.

_____. *The War for Korea. Vol. 2: 1950–1951: They Came from the North.* Lawrence: University Press of Kansas, 2010. In this and the preceding volume, an eminent military historian covers the long prologue to the Korean War, starting with Korea's liberation from Japan and the development of South Korean society and institutions under American guidance. Emphasis on the growth of the military and Korea's emergence as a surrogate in the cold war. Both volumes draw on the author's deep knowledge of military cultures in the U.S.-Korean alliance, including long acquaintance with military leaders on both sides.

Oberdorfer, Don. *The Two Koreas.* New York: Basic Books, 2002. A longtime *Washington Post* correspondent and Korea scholar at the Johns Hopkins School for Advanced International Studies (SAIS) offers a thorough political history of South and North Korea. Especially detailed for the later Park years and the transition to democracy in South Korea, as well as the nuclear "crisis" of the 1990s and North Korea's troubled efforts to deal with the multiple challenges of life after the collapse of communism in Eastern Europe and the Soviet Union and the passing of Kim Il-sung.

Robinson, Michael Edson. *Korea's Twentieth Century Odyssey.*
Honolulu: University of Hawai'i Press, 2007. A compact text
organized expressly for classroom use, with evenhanded treatments
of major movements and episodes in the development of modern
Korea. Especially strong on the Japanese colonial period and the
development of the Republic of Korea.

NORTH KOREA

Hassig, Ralph, and Kongdan Oh. *The Hidden People of North Korea:
Life in the Hermit Kingdom.* Lanham, Md.: Rowman and Littlefield,
2009. In their second book on North Korea, Hassig and Oh examine
the various levels of caste, the daily economy, and the decaying
infrastructure of life in the DPRK. They do not spare the leadership
as they show what sustains the system for the time being, how it is
changing despite all efforts to fend off "reforms," and its ultimate
unsustainability.

Lankov, Andrei. *North of the DMZ: Essays on Daily Life in North
Korea.* Jefferson, N.C.: McFarland, 2007. Russian scholar Andrei
Lankov, who once participated in North Korean life as a student
at Kim Il-sung University and now teaches in South Korea and
Australia, offers an array of interpretative essays on life in the
DPRK. He writes, "Even under the most repressive of social and
political conditions, the vast majority of people still attempt to live
normal lives and generally succeed at it." Lankov confronts the fact
that the world sees North Korea as a major threat when actually it is
"nothing but a small and grossly underdeveloped dictatorship, whose
population size and major economic indicators are roughly similar to
those of Mozambique." Accordingly, *North of the DMZ* is "about the
world the North Koreans themselves have created and have to live
in." The essays are human, fascinating, often tragic, full of detail and
insight, and ultimately an intelligent grasp of what reality is to the
North Koreans.

Martin, Bradley. *Under the Loving Care of the Fatherly Leader.*
New York: St. Martin's Griffin, 2006. Long based in Asia as one of
America's leading journalists, Bradley Martin struggles with the
experience of multiple visits to the DPRK as an outsider subjected to
the limits and relentless propaganda output of the Kim regime. His
background enables him to place this in the wider context of world
politics and economics. The book uses many Korean voices, officials

north and south, and refugees and /defectors, as well as country specialists and "sources," to bring depth to the study. What develops is a well-colored snapshot of the North Korean system in the 2000s.

Myers, B. R. *The Cleanest Race: How North Koreans See Themselves and Why It Matters.* Brooklyn: Melvin House, 2010. Myers, a scholar of North Korean literature, shares insights into the worldview of North Koreans, explaining their nationalism in terms of racial purity and a childlike dependence on a "mother" state. He sees this less as Confucian than as a continuation of Japanese imperial notions of the organic state. The self-image of North Korea as vulnerable requires citizens to sacrifice everything if necessary to maintain their "family."

Portal, Jane. *Art under Control in North Korea.* London: Reaktion Books, 2006. The author, who developed the Korean collection at the British Museum and now chairs the Asian art department at the Boston Museum of Fine Arts, approaches the DPRK through its symbols and paintings. She reveals some of what the North Korean system is trying to inspire via its manipulations of socialist realism and monumental buildings, arches, statues, stadiums, slogans, towers, and other overpowering Kimilsungist constructions. Her treatment unpacks North Korea's artistic debts to Korean tradition as well as socialist realism, Chinese and Soviet communism, modern Western perspectives, and North Korea's own manufactured story.